Eyewitness Accounts of the American Revolution

Journal of
Charles Carroll, 1776

The New York Times & Arno Press

Memorial Contribution

FROM THE

Maryland Historical Society,

TO THE

CENTENNIAL CELEBRATION

OF THE

NATIONAL INDEPENDENCE

OF THE

UNITED STATES OF AMERICA,

JULY 4TH, 1876.

Painted by McLaty. Eng^d by H.B.Hall.

CHARLES CARROLL of CARROLLTON.

JOURNAL

OF

Charles Carroll of Carrollton,

DURING HIS

Visit to Canada in 1776,

AS ONE OF THE COMMISSIONERS FROM CONGRESS;

WITH A MEMOIR AND NOTES.

BY BRANTZ MAYER.

PRINTED BY JOHN MURPHY,

FOR THE MARYLAND HISTORICAL SOCIETY,

BALTIMORE, MAY, 1876.

The Maryland Historical Society wishing to bring a proper offering to the first Centennial Celebration of our National Indedendence, resolved, foɪ that purpose, to reprint a Journal of Charles Carroll of Carrollton, of Maryland, signer of the Declaration of Independence. The original manuscript of this record is kept in the Archives of the Society as a precious gift from the descendants of its illustrious author.

The Journal was written by Mr. Carroll, in 1776, during a journey to Canada with Benjamin Franklin of Pennsylvania, and Samuel Chase of Maryland, members of Congress, and,— jointly with Mr. Carroll,—its delegated Commissioners to try the feeling, and, if possible, to stir up the Canadians. By the request of Congress the Reverend John Carroll, cousin of Charles Carroll of Carrollton, and afterwards, the first Roman Catholic Archbishop of the United States, accompanied these gentlemen on their grave and delicate errand.

The undersigned were named by the Society to carry out its wishes; and with great respect, they offer this book as a patriotic memorial—showing that, at the end of one hundred years of National life, Maryland is loyal to the men and memories of 1776.

BRANTZ MAYER,

WILLIAM H. CORNER,

JOHN J. JACOBSEN,

Committee of the Maryland Historical Society.

BALTIMORE, *Maryland*, 1 May, 1876.

INTRODUCTORY MEMOIR

UPON THE

EXPEDITION TO CANADA

IN

1775–1776.

CHAPTER I.

THAT long line of lakes and rivers which flow southeastwardly across our continent, and empty into the Atlantic through the gulf of Saint Lawrence, seems to form a natural barrier between two nations, marking their geographical limits if it did not also bound different races. And such, in fact, was really the case with a part of this extensive chain, until the peace of Paris in 1763, when Canada, after the victory of Wolfe, passed from the dominion of France to that of the British crown.

In March, 1766, the stamp act was repealed; but the English ministry, foiled in its first attempt

on the liberties of the American colonies, seemed
determined to tease and worry them into rebellion. Taxation by duties was laid in 1767, and
Maryland at once took ground against the imposi-
tion. Associations for "non importation" were
speedily formed; but, after existing for a while,
they were abandoned, and local discontents arose
in our state that exasperated the people's feelings
against Ministerial oppressions, until they were
ripe for the revolt that ultimately broke out.[1]

Amongst the earliest demonstrations of a disposition on the part of the colonists to resort to
violence, was the attack upon the newly ceded
province of Canada.

The expedition that was sent to the north was
deemed, by some persons, of questionable policy,
and not a few of our people thought it entirely
subversive of the principles upon which we
grounded our resistance. It might naturally,
they alleged, be regarded as a *war of conquest*,
and, as such, was entirely at variance with the
spirit of our discontent.

Such, however, was not a just view of the case.
The boundary of the lakes to which we have
alluded, formed, in reality, no boundary to British
rule, for the sway of the Anglo-Saxon race was
now fully established over the whole of the north-

[1] See McMahon's History of Maryland, vol. i, p. 380.

ern part of the continent. It was obviously
proper, therefore, to detract, if possible, from the
power of our assailants to harm us on the great
watery highway of the lakes and rivers, or to
present such an united force of colonial and pro-
vincial inhabitants as might counterbalance, in
a great measure, the pertinacious loyalists who
were disposed to discountenance our appeals for
justice. For it will be remembered, that before
the declaration of our national independence, the
warfare was neither against the throne nor the
laws of England, but against a reckless and op-
pressive ministry.[1]

In taking advantage, therefore, of this general
desire to enlist the whole of the British subjects
in America in the preservation of their privileges,
efforts were justly and fairly made to obtain
possession of the keys of the lakes and of the
St. Lawrence at Quebec and Montreal.

As Sir Guy Carleton had manifested a strong
disposition to sustain the ministry against the
people, it was hoped that his efforts would thus
be neutralized, and an unbroken front of firm and
resisting freemen presented to the cabinet and
parliament.

Canada was a province whose citizens had not
yet coalesced with the English. In the debate on

[1] See Col. Reed's letter to Washington, and Washington's reply.—
Washington's Writings, vol. iii, p. 347.

the Canada bill, in 1774, the widest latitude of
opinion was expressed as to the proper government and laws for the conquered province, and
the most lamentable ignorance was displayed as
to the character and temper of the people.[1]

Under the French the spirit of the government
had been military. Conquest was the chief object,
and the desire of the authorities was to command
the lakes, to control the territories on the Ohio,
and thus, descending the Mississippi to Louisiana;
to embrace the great internal resources of this
continent by two gigantic arms, one of which
should rest on the St. Lawrence whilst the other
controlled the Gulf of Mexico. Canada, therefore,
was the citadel and nursery of their troops. Large
detachments were sent every year to the Ohio and
to other interior parts of North America, and, by
these annual campaigns, the province was drained
of its blood and energy. The people had no time
for settlement and its peaceful results. Marriages
were prevented, and numbers perished in the toil-
some services to which they were devoted among
the savages of the remote wilderness. But, after
the conquest by Great Britain, the aspect of affairs
was changed. The government became one of
peace, and the inhabitants—not greatly augmented
in numbers by emigration — were permitted to

[1] See Cavendish's Debates on the Canada bill in 1774.

cultivate their lands, whilst the judges took care not to interfere essentially with their laws and customs.[1] Besides this, the policy of England towards Canada was wise in another respect. In October, 1763, a royal proclamation was made, by which the province of Quebec was limited and bounded; and on the 13th of June, 1774, parliament passed the "Quebec act," by which those limits were enlarged, and his majesty's subjects professing the religion of the church of Rome, were guarantied the free exercise of their worship, whilst their priests were protected in the full discharge of all their functions.

Thus Canada, though a *quasi* foreign country, was a contented one, and it behooved our statesmen to take heed lest her people, still alive to their ancient military glory, might annoy or distract our frontier. The warfare, therefore, that we waged within her borders, was one, in fact, of political propagandism, in which the people, unfortunately for themselves as the sequel proved, took but little interest.

We will not dwell on the successes of our troops in Canada up to the spring of 1776. So many works have been written on the history of that period and on the biography of the eminent men who led our armies, that it would be useless, in

[1] See " Debates," &c., pp. 104, 105.

this sketch, to review the earlier part of our campaign.

But after the successes of Arnold and Allen at Ticonderoga and Crown Point, the former of these officers pushed on towards Quebec through the wilderness. By the capture of a small fleet at Sorel, under General Prescott, the Americans had gained command of the St. Lawrence above Quebec, and, as all the British posts in Canada were under our control, except the capital, that now became the object of eager enterprise.[1]

On the 31st of December, 1775, Montgomery stormed that stronghold, and fell in the attack. Our troops were unsuccessful in effecting a lodgment; but Arnold, on whom the command devolved, sat down resolutely before the capital, in the depth of winter, and with the small remnant of his troops besieged a Ministerial army of nearly double his number.

Reinforcements were sent to our colonial general, who had been immediately promoted for his gallantry, and troops that carried their own provisions during a perilous march on snow shoes, through the forests, reached him from Vermont, New Hampshire, and Massachusetts.

With this fragmentary, undisciplined, ill-fed, and miserable array, he kept his ground until

[1] See Sparks's Life of Arnold.

spring. Meanwhile, Wooster had quietly rested during the long and severe winter, in the secure and undisputed Montreal. "A state of repose," says Mr. Sparks, "which his countrymen were not prepared to expect from a man who had gained the reputation of a bold and active officer in the last war."[1]

However, on the 1st of April, 1776, he left his winter quarters for Quebec, and, as he outranked Arnold, took command immediately on his arrival. Arnold, who was no doubt discontented at not being permitted to continue in authority at a season when he might have struck a daring and effectual blow, forthwith departed for Montreal, and left this weak and injudicious officer to conduct the siege.[2]

Canada was thus, in fact, in the possession of our colonial troops, yet the tenure was rather nominal than real. It was a conflict between *the military* on both sides, whilst *the people* of the province—the subject matter of all available controversy—had as yet manifested no ardent desire to join us.

Such was the state of things early in the memorable year of '76. But the feeble grasp with which we held that remote province was not long to be continued. On the first of April, Col. Hazen, who

---

[1] See Sparks's Life of Arnold, p. 55.

[2] See Mr. Carroll's Journal, of the 25th of May, and note, for the Commissioners' opinion of Wooster's conduct in Canada.

had taken command at Montreal, on the departure
of General Wooster, and before the arrival of
Arnold, thus wrote to General Schuyler:

"You are not unacquainted with the friendly
disposition of the Canadians when General Montgomery first penetrated into the country. The
ready assistance they gave on all occasions, by
men, carriages, or provisions, was most remarkable. Even when he was before Quebec, many
parishes offered their services in the reduction of
that fortress, which were at that time thought
unnecessary. But his most unfortunate fate, added
to other incidents, has caused such a change in
their disposition, that we no longer look upon
them as friends, but, on the contrary, as waiting
an opportunity to join our enemies. That no
observations of my own may remain obscure, I
beg leave to observe that I think the clergy, or
guardians of the souls and conductors of the bodies
of these enthusiasts, have been neglected, perhaps,
in some instances, ill used. Be that as it will, they
are unanimous, though privately, against our cause,
and I have too much reason to fear that many of
them, with other people of some consequence, have
carried on a correspondence the whole winter with
General Carleton in Quebec, and are now plotting
our destruction. The peasantry in general have
been ill used. They have, in some instances, been
dragooned with the point of the bayonet to supply

wood for the garrison at a lower rate than the current price. For carriages and many other articles furnished, illegible certificates have been given without signature; the one-half, of consequence, rejected by the quartermaster-general. It is true, payment has been promised from time to time; yet they look upon such promises as vague, their labor and property lost, and the congress or United Colonies bankrupt. And, in a more material point, they have not seen sufficient force in the country to protect them. These matters furnish very strong arguments to be made use of by our enemies. With respect to the better sort of people, both French and English, seven-eighths are tories, who would wish to see our throats cut, and perhaps would readily assist in doing it.

"You may remember, sir, in a conversation with you at Albany, I urged the necessity of sending immediately to Canada able generals, a respectable army, a committee of congress, a suitable supply of hard cash, and a printer. Indeed, I had before represented those measures in person to congress, at least, to the committee of congress, and we have since been flattered, from time to time, that we should have one or all of these essentials."[1]

The commissioners, alluded to by Colonel Hazen, had already been appointed by congress; and, on

---

[1] See Washington's Writings, vol, iii, p. 361, note.

3

the day subsequent to the date of his letter, had departed from the city of New York on their way to Montreal.

On the 15th of February, '76, it was "Resolved that a committee of three—two of whom to be members of congress—be appointed to repair to Canada, there to pursue such instructions as shall be given them by that body."[1]

Dr. BENJAMIN FRANKLIN, SAMUEL CHASE, and CHAS. CARROLL of Carrollton,[2] were chosen for this purpose (the two first named being members), and, by a special resolution, the last mentioned gentleman was desired "to prevail on Mr. JOHN CARROLL to accompany the committee to Canada to assist them in such matters as they shall think useful."

This gentleman, who afterwards became the first Roman Catholic Archbishop of the United States, had already received holy orders in Europe. He was a Jesuit of distinguished theological attainments, and was celebrated for his amiable manners and polished address. Both of the Carrolls were educated in Europe, and had formed connections of the most intimate kind with the people of the old world. The Rev. John Carroll had been private

---

[1] See Journals of Congress, vol. ii, p. 62, edition of 1800.

[2] Charles Carroll of Carrollton was elected a member of the Congress by the Maryland Convention on the 4th of July, 1776, and took his seat on the 18th. He signed the Declaration of Independence on the 12th of August, 1776.

tutor in the family of Lord Stourton, with whom he made the tour of Europe after the dissolution of the Jesuits, and might, therefore, have been supposed to lean to the side of loyalty; but all the members of his family had early manifested their partiality for the colonies. Mr. Charles Carroll of of Carrollton, also a Roman Catholic, after finishing his studies in the Temple and returning to Maryland, had distinguished himself by his controversy with DANIEL DULANY, the great legal luminary of Maryland, on the proclamation and vestry questions,[1] and had intimated his resolution to sustain his native land against the oppressions of the mother country. The one was an humble but learned clergyman; the other an independent lawyer of ample fortune and promising talents; but both staked, at once, their lives and honor on the issues of the day, and were thus prepared to take conspicuous parts in the approaching revolution.

Whilst congress was anxious to aid the cool judgment of Franklin by the intrepidity of Chase and the courtly address of Carroll, it went still further, and requested the polished churchman to unite himself with the expedition, "and assist the commissioners in such things as they might think useful." The object of this, although not entered

[1] See McMahon's History of Maryland, vol. i, p. 388, and Green's Gazette, 1773.

on the journals of congress or expressed in any formal preamble to the resolutions, is perfectly evident. In the debates on the Canada bill, in 1774, we are informed that there were one hundred and fifty thousand Catholics, and only three hundred and sixty Protestants within the government of the province of Quebec,[1] and it was therefore believed that one of the surest means of prompt success with such a mass of Roman Catholics, was to show them, by influential men of their own creed, that their brethren over the border, were up in arms and ready to do battle in defence of religious and political liberty. Three of these representatives came from a province originally founded by tolerant Catholics, who had received a tolerant charter even from a bigoted king.[2]

We have seen that the Rev. Mr. Carroll was an undoubted patriot, agreeing with the liberals in all their views; yet it might be asserted that he was

---

[1] See Debates, &c., p. 103.

[2] We hold the opinion that no act could have been legally passed by our colonial legislature in Maryland, in conformity with the charter of Charles, that was not TOLERANT in its character to all religionists. Our opinion is founded on a clause in the twenty-second section of that instrument, which declares that the charter shall be expounded always in the most favorable and beneficial manner for the benefit of Lord Baltimore, his heirs and assigns,—" Proviso semper quod nulla fiat interpretatio per quam sacro-sancta Dei et vera *Christiana religio* aut Ligeantia nobis hæredibus et successoribus nostris debita immutatione prejudicio vel dispendio in aliquo patiantur eo quod expressa mentis," &c.

Broad Christianity alone is here referred to, and that was not to suffer by "change, prejudice, or diminution."

not justified in joining an expedition that would kindle the flame of religious war on the Catholic frontier. Such, certainly, was also Mr. Carroll's opinion, and he felt, as deeply as any man in the colonies that religion should never become an auxiliary of strife, and that it was his duty, as a clergyman, to allay, if possible, the angry spirit of the times and to prevail on the disaffected subjects of Britain to maintain their allegiance by presenting a bold front to Ministerial misrule.

In order, therefore, to estimate the delicacy of Mr. Carroll's position, we must recollect that at the period when congress required his services, the prospect of reconciliation with the king was not entirely shut out. Appeals, protests, and remonstrances had been tried in vain. All the ordinary efforts of *persuasion* had failed to produce redress. In such a state of things it would seem but reasonable that a patriotic priest, who regarded his duty to his country as next to that he owed to God, and who was zealous for the religious as well as the political freedom of his brethren, should seize upon so favorable an occasion to render service of lasting value to the large, conquered mass of Canadian Catholics. He was, perhaps, about to obtain a boon for himself; he desired that others should participate in its benefits. And he naturally felt anxious that, when civil and religious liberty were for ever secured to the colonies, the subjects north of the lakes should, at the same time, obtain a permanent concession of fair and equal laws.

Mr. Carroll was, therefore, very properly desirous to identify Canada with our struggle or to procure her neutrality; as, from her imposing size, her commanding geographical position, her foreign population, and her recent disruption from France, —her resolved attitude of defiance or indifference would, in all probability, strike terror into the minds of the headstrong Ministry; and thus, by opposing the formidable animosity of a United Continent, we should gain our ends and nip the war in its ripening bud.[1] Mr. Carroll's views, therefore, were eminently pacific, and their wisdom has since been fully proved. The colonies obtained their independence, whilst Canada remains a discontented, refractory province of the British empire.[2]

---

[1] See the Baltimore U. S. Catholic Magazine, vol. iv, page 251, and Brent's Biography of Archbishop Carroll, p. 69.

[2] One of the writer's earliest recollections is of the funeral of this excellent prelate, which was celebrated with great pomp at Baltimore, in 1815, and attended by citizens of all Christian denominations. The loss of Archbishop Carroll was not a loss alone to the church over which he presided and which he may be said to have founded in the United States. Men of all creeds loved him, for his life had been one of tolerance, charity, and affection. His career, as priest and prelate, had been conceived in that spirit of Christian moderation which, whilst it upheld firmly the truth and efficacy of his own creed, still regarded the professors of other forms as entitled to a liberal and unbigoted consideration. This good bishop, who was long mourned, and will be long remembered by Marylanders, died in this city, at the age of eighty, on the 3d of December, 1815.

It is worthy of special note that Dr. Franklin, who now, at the advanced age of seventy, was sent on this fatiguing journey to wrest Canada from England or neutralize it, had been seventeen years before, one of the first to urge its conquest upon the mother country. When he was in London in 1759, although he had no interviews with the minister, his conversation on American affairs was always respectfully heeded by men in power, and "it has been said on good authority," declares Mr. Sparks, "that the expedition against Canada, and its consequences in the victory of Wolfe at Quebec and the conquest of that country, may be chiefly ascribed to Franklin. He disapproved the policy, by which the ministry had hitherto been guided, of carrying on the war against the French in the heart of Germany, where, if successful, it would end in no real gain to the British nation, and no essential loss to the enemy. In all companies and on all occasions, he urged the reduction of Canada as an object of the utmost importance. It would inflict a blow upon the French power in America from which it could never recover, and which would have a lasting influence in advancing the prosperity of the British Colonies. These sentiments he conveyed to the minister's friends, with such remarks on the practicability of the enterprise, and the manner of conducting it, as his intimate knowledge of the state of things

in America enabled him to communicate. They
made the impression he desired, and the result
verified his prediction."[1]

The same ripe judgment that discerned the importance of Canada for England, in order to give
her control over the lakes and the west, adopted
it for the colonies also, and thus Franklin was
discreetly selected for this responsible mission.

CHAPTER II.

ON the 2d of April, 1776, FRANKLIN, CHASE,
and the Carrolls, properly equipped for so fatiguing a journey of more than four hundred miles,
departed from the city of New York in a sloop
for Albany.

These gentlemen had, of course, been duly com-
missioned by congress "to promote or to form a
union between the colonies and the people of
Canada;" and on the 20th of March, they received their ample instructions.

They were told to represent to the Canadians
that the arms of the United Colonies had been
carried into that province for the purpose of frus-

[1] Sparks's Writings, vol. i, pp. 248, 257.

trating the designs of the British court against our common liberties; that we expected not only to defeat the hostile machinations of Governor Carleton against us, but that we should put it in the power of our Canadian brethren to pursue such measures for securing their own freedom and happiness as a generous love of liberty and sound policy should dictate to them.

They were desired to inform them that, in the judgment of congress, their interest and that of the colonies were inseparably united. That it was impossible we could be reduced to a servile submission to Great Britain without their sharing in our fate; and, on the other hand, if we obtained, as we doubted not we should, a full establishment of our rights, it depended wholly on *their* choice, whether they would participate with us in those blessings, or still remain subject to every act of tyranny which British ministers should please to exercise over them.

They were told to urge all such arguments as their prudence suggested to enforce our opinion concerning the mutual interests of the two countries, and to convince them of the impossibility of the war being concluded to the disadvantage of the colonies, if we wisely and vigorously co-operated with each other. To convince them of the uprightness of our intentions towards them, they were to declare that it was the inclination

4

of congress that the people of Canada should set
up such a form of government as would be most
likely, in their judgment, to promote their happiness. And they were, in the strongest terms, to
assure them that it was our earnest desire to adopt
them into our union as a sister colony, and to
secure the same system of mild and equal laws
for them and for ourselves, with only such local
differences as might be agreeable to each colony
respectively.

They were to assure the Canadians that we had
no apprehension *that the French would take any part
with Great Britain; but that it was their interest, and,
we had reason to believe, their inclination, to cultivate a
friendly intercourse with these colonies.*

From this and such other reasons as might
appear most proper, they were charged to urge
the necessity the people were under of immediately taking some decisive step to put themselves
within the protection of the United Colonies. For
expediting such a measure, they were to explain
our method of collecting the sense of the people
and conducting our affairs regularly by committees
of observation and inspection in the several dis-
tricts, and by conventions and committees of safety
in the several colonies. These modes were to be
recommended to them. The nature and principles
of government among freemen were to be fully
explained, developing, in contrast to these, the

base, cruel, and insidious designs involved in the late act of parliament for making a more effectual provision for the government of the province of Quebec.[1] Motives of glory and interest were to be proposed as stimulants to the Canadians to unite in a contest by which they must be deeply affected, *and they were to be taught to aspire to a portion of that power by which they were ruled, and not to remain the mere spoils and prey of their conquerors.*

They were directed, further, to declare that *we held sacred the rights of conscience; and should promise to the whole people, solemnly, in the name of congress, the free and undisturbed exercise of their religion; and to the clergy the full, perfect, and peaceable possession and enjoyment of all their estates:—that the government of every thing relative to their creed and clergy should be left, entirely, in the hands of the good people of that province, and such legislature as they should constitute; provided, however, that all other denominations of Christians should be equally entitled to hold offices, and enjoy civil privileges and the free exercise of their religion, as well as be totally exempt from the payment of any tithes or taxes for the support of religion.*

They were desired to press for a convention of the people, a speedy organization of government,

---

[1] The "Quebec act," passed June, 1774.

and union with the colonies. The terms of the
union should be similar to those of the other
colonies; and, if our terms were acceded to, they
were to promise our defence of the Canadians
against all enemies.

A free press was to be established, and the commissioners were to settle all disputes betwixt the
Canadians and continental troops. They were to
reform all abuses, to enforce peace and good order,
and were empowered to sit and vote in councils of
war; to erect or demolish fortifications, and to
suspend military officers from the exercise of their
commissions until the pleasure of congress should
be known.

In additional instructions, they were empowered
and directed to encourage the trade of Canada with
the Indians, and to assure the Canadians that their
foreign commerce should be put on the same footing
as that of the United Colonies.[1]

Armed with their commission and these instructions, our travellers departed, as we have seen, on
the 2d of April, from the city of New York; but it
was not until the 29th—nearly a month afterwards
—that they reached their destination at Montreal.
The details of this expedition will be found in the
accompanying diary of Mr. Carroll of Carrollton,
and the reader can not fail to be pleased with

---

[1] See these instructions at large in the Amer. Archives, vol. v, p. 411.

the patient and interesting narrative of the journalist.

It seems from this document, and the correspondence of Franklin, that the Doctor remained in Montreal until the 11th of May,—a few days only after the abandonment of Quebec by our troops,—and was joined, on the following morning, by the Rev. Mr. John Carroll at St. Johns. Dr. Franklin's health had suffered greatly by the journey, and he soon perceived that his efforts in Canada would be of no avail. On the contrary, he saw that public opinion was setting strongly against the colonies, that the army was in a wretched condition, that the mouth of the St. Lawrence was lost, and that powerful reinforcements would probably soon arrive from abroad. He therefore left Canada to younger and more hopeful men, and departed with his clerical friend, who had been equally unsuccessful.

The object of this mission was doubtless twofold: first, to induce the Catholics to join us, or remain neutral; and secondly, to make such military demonstrations as would secure us the province *in spite of its people*. To the first of these objects the Rev. Mr. Carroll immediately addressed himself, and it seems that, within ten days after his arrival in Montreal, all his diplomacy proved ineffectual.

"While the commissioners were applying them-selves," says Mr. Campbell in his excellent me-moir,[1] "with their characteristic ardor to the fulfilment of their trust, the Rev. Mr. Carroll, whose exertions were of a different character, was diligently employed in visiting the clergy, and conferring with individuals among them. He ex-plained to them the nature of the differences between England and the United Colonies, show-ing that the resistance of the latter was caused by invasions of their charters, and violations of well known and long recognized principles of the British constitution. To this the clergy replied that, since the acquisition of Canada by the British government, its inhabitants had no agressions to complain of; that, on the contrary, government had faithfully complied with all the stipulations of the treaty, and had in fact sanctioned and pro-tected the ancient laws and customs of Canada, even so far as to allow the French judicial or-ganization and forms of law, with a delicacy that demanded their respect and gratitude. The

[1] See Life and Times of Archbishop Carroll, by B. U. Campbell.— *U. S. Catholic Magazine*, vol. iii, p. 244, &c.

Mr. Campbell states, in a letter to me, that "the part taken by the Rev. Mr. Carroll in Canada was communicated to him by Dr. Fenwick, bishop of Boston, a personal friend of Archbishop Caroll, who, in a visit to Canada, met an aged Canadian priest who had seen Dr. Carroll there, and gave Dr. Fenwick an account of what passed between Dr. Carroll and the Canadian clergy, with his disapprobation of the course of Dr. Carroll in endeavoring to enlist the Catholic clergy on the side of the United Colonies."

Rev. Mr. Carroll then represented to them that congress had expressly stipulated that if the Canadians would unite with the colonies in the assertion of their constitutional rights, their religion, its institutions, and the property of the religious orders and communities should be protected and guarantied; and that Catholics, instead of being merely tolerated as by England, should have equal rights with the professors of all other religions. To these assurances the Canadians replied that, on the score of religious liberty, the British government had left them nothing to complain of or to desire; that they were then in possession of all the ecclesiastical property which they had held at the time of the cession of Canada, that their numerous and important missions were flourishing, and their religious societies felt entire confidence in the protection of the government, whose officers carried their courtesy and respect so far as to pay military honors to the public religious exercises, a conspicuous evidence of which was, that the government actually furnished a military escort to accompany the grand processions on the festival of Corpus Christi. And, therefore, that upon the well established principle that allegiance is due to protection, the clergy could not teach that neutrality was consistent with the allegiance due to such ample protection as Great Britain had shown the Catholics of Canada.

"The judicious and liberal policy of the British government to the Catholics had succeeded in inspiring them with sentiments of loyalty, which the conduct of the people and the public bodies of some of the United Colonies had served to strengthen and confirm. It was remembered, and stated to the Rev. Mr. Carroll, that in the colonies whose liberality he was now avouching, the Catholic religion had not been tolerated hitherto. Priests were excluded under severe penalties, and Catholic missionaries among the Indians rudely and cruelly treated. His explanation that these harsh measures were the result, in a great part, of the laws of the royal government, did not satisfy the Canadians of the favorable dispositions of those who, though prompt and valiant in the defence of their political rights, had never manifested a correspondent sensibility in support of the sacred rights of conscience when Catholics were concerned. The friends of the royal government had assiduously pointed out inconsistencies between the address of the continental congress to the people of Great Britain and that addressed to the people of Canada.

"By the 'Quebec act,' passed by parliament, it was provided that his majesty's subjects professing the religion of the church of Rome, of and in the said province of Quebec, may have, hold, and enjoy the free exercise of the religion of the church of Rome, &c., and that the clergy of the said church may hold, receive, and enjoy their accustomed dues and rights, with respect to such persons only as shall profess the said religion. They were also excused from taking the oath required by the statute of 1st Elizabeth, or any other oath substituted by other acts in the place thereof, &c.

"Unfortunately, the address of congress to the people of Great Britain, adopted the 21st of October, 1774, had used the following language in reference to the 'Quebec act:'

" 'Nor can we suppress our astonishment that a British parliament should ever consent to establish in that country a religion that has deluged your island in blood, and dispersed impiety, bigotry, persecution, murder, and rebellion through every part of the world.' And 'that we think the legislature of Great Britain is not authorized by the constitution to establish a religion fraught with sanguinary and impious tenets,' &c.

"After sentiments which did their religion so much injustice, the Canadian clergy were not disposed to receive with much favor the following declarations of the same congress in their 'Address to the inhabitants of the province of Quebec:' 'We are too well acquainted with the liberality of sentiment distinguishing your nation, to imagine that difference of religion will preju-

5

dice you against a hearty amity with us. You
know that the transcendent nature of freedom
elevates those who unite in her cause above all
such low-minded infirmities. The Swiss cantons
furnish a memorable proof of this truth. Their
union is composed of Roman Catholic and Pro-
testant states, living in the utmost concord and
peace with one another, and thereby enabled,
ever since they bravely vindicated their freedom,
to defy and defeat every tyrant that has in-
vaded them.'"[1]

The Rev. Mr. Carroll, having thus failed in his
part of the mission, joined Dr. Franklin and returned to the south. Meanwhile, however, Messrs.
Chase and Carroll of Carrollton had been busy

[1] "Nothing can exhibit more clearly the bad effects, upon the Canadians, of the address to the British people, than the following contempo-
raneous letter, comprised among the revolutionary documents recently
published by order of congress.

"Extract of a letter from Canada, dated Montreal, March 24, 1775.

"'The address from the Continental Congress attracted the notice of
some of the principal Canadians; it was soon translated into very
tolerable French. The decent manner in which the religious matters
were touched, the encomiums on the French nation, flattered a people fond
of compliments. They begged the translator, as he had succeeded so
well, to try his hand on that addressed to Great Britain. He had equal
success in this, and read his performance to a numerous audience. But
when he came to that part which treats of the new modeling of the
province, draws a picture of the Catholic religion, and Canadian manners, they could not contain their resentment, nor express it but in
broken curses. 'O the perfidious double-faced Congress! Let us bless
and obey our benevolent Prince, whose humanity is consistent, and extends to all religions; let us abhor all who would seduce us from our
loyalty, by acts that would dishonor a Jesuit, and whose addresses, like
their resolves, are destructive of their own objects.'"—*American Archives,*
vol. ii, p. 231.

Eng.d by HB Hall.

Painted by Jarvis.

SAMUEL CHASE.

with the military part of their embassy. On the day after their arrival at Montreal, they attended a council of war,[1] in which it was resolved to fortify Jacques Cartier,—the Falls of Richelieu, an important post between Quebec and Montreal, —and to build six gondolas at Chamblay, of a proper size to carry heavy cannon, and to be under the direction of Arnold. But disasters thickened around the insurgents. The small-pox had broken out among the troops, and was making deep inroads upon their scanty num-bers. The Canadians showed no symptoms of sympathy with the colonists, and, to crown the whole, bad news was soon received from the be-siegers at Quebec.

On the 1st of May, General Thomas had taken command at the capital, and found by the returns that, out of nineteen hundred men, there were not more than a thousand, including officers, who were fit for duty; all the rest were invalids, chiefly afflicted with smallpox. There were several posts to be defended by this trifling force, and at such distances from each other that not more than three hundred men could be rallied to the relief of any one of them, should it be assailed by the whole force of the enemy. Besides this, there were but one hundred and fifty pounds of powder, and only

---

[1] See American Archives, vol. v, p. 1166.

six days' provisions in the camp, whilst their French neighbors were so disaffected towards the colonists that supplies were procured with the greatest difficulty.

On the fifth, a council of war was held, and it was resolved to remove the invalids, artillery, batteaux, and stores higher up the river, so as to prevent our being cut off by water from the interior posts in the event of the arrival of reinforcements to the enemy. But, on the evening of the same day, intelligence was received in the American camp that fifteen ships were forty leagues below Quebec, hastening up the river; and early next morning five of them hove in sight.

General Thomas[1] immediately gave orders to embark the artillery and sick in the batteaux, whilst the enemy began to land their troops. About noon a body of the British, a thousand strong, formed into two divisions in columns of six deep, and supported with a train of six pieces of cannon, attacked our sentinels and main guard. Our officers made a stand for a moment on the plains, with about two hundred and fifty men and *one* field piece only, when the order for retreat was given and our encampment was precipitately deserted. In the confusion all our cannon and

---

[1] He died of smallpox soon after the retreat to Sorel.

ammunition fell into the enemy's hands, and it is believed that about two hundred of our invalids were made prisoners. Following the course of the river, our broken army fled towards Montreal, and, halting for a while at Deschambault, finally retreated along the St. Lawrence, until it made a stand at Sorel.[1] And thus Quebec was lost for ever to the colonists.

Meantime the commissioners had kept up a faithful correspondence with congress, and they continued it until their departure from Canada. Their manuscript letters, preserved in the department at Washington, are dated on the 1st, 8th, 10th, 16th, and 27th of May.[2] The last of these, perhaps, is the most interesting of the series, and, as it gives the results of their examinations, we shall let it speak for itself, especially as the "written report" made to congress by Messrs. Chase and Carroll, on the 12th of June, 1776, could not with the most diligent search be found in Washington.

---

[1] See the letters of General Thomas to the Commissioners, May 7th, 1776; and of General Arnold to General Schuyler, May 10, 1776.— *American Archives*, vol. vi, pp. 451, 452.

[2] See American Archives, vols. v and vi.

"*Montreal*, 27*th May*, 1776.

"THE COMMISSIONERS IN CANADA
  "TO THE PRESIDENT OF CONGRESS:

*　*　*　*　*　*　*　*　*　*

"In our last we informed you of the deplorable state of the army; matters have not mended since. We went to the mouth of *Sorel* last week, where we found all things in confusion; there is little or no discipline among your troops, nor can any be kept up while the practice of enlisting for a twelve-month continues; the general officers are all of this opinion. *Your army is badly paid; and so exhausted is your credit that even a cart can not be procured without ready money or force.* We will give you an instance of the lowness of your credit. Three barrels of gunpowder were ordered from *Chamblay* to *Montreal;* this powder was brought from *Chamblay* to a ferry, about three miles off, where it would have remained had we not luckily passed by, and, seeing the distress of the officer, undertaken to pay ready and hard money for the hire of a cart to convey it to *Longueil.* The army is in a distressed condition, and is in want of the most necessary articles—meat, bread, tents, shoes, stockings, shirts, &c. The greatest part of those who fled from *Quebec* left all their baggage behind them, or it was plundered by those whose times were out, and have since left *Canada*. We are informed by Colonel *Allen that the men who, from pretended indisposition, had been excused from doing duty, were the foremost in the flight, and carried off such burdens on their backs as hearty and stout men would labor under.*

"With difficulty three hundred tents, and about two hundred camp-kettles, were procured here, and sent to the *Sorel* for the use of the army, and were delivered, as we were informed, to one Major *Fuller*, who acted in the room of Mr. *Campbell*, deputy quartermaster-general, who had joined the army at the *Sorel* but a day or two before our arrival, where, among other instances of mismanagement, we give the following: Colonel *Nicholson's* regiment, consisting only of one hundred men, received thirty tents and thirty-one camp-kettles; Colonel *Porter's* regiment, not exceeding that number, received fifty-six tents and thirty-three kettles.

"Your army in *Canada* do not exceed four thousand; above four hundred are sick with different disorders; *three-fourths of the army have not had the smallpox.* The greater part of *Greaton's, Bond's,* and *Burrell's* regiments have been lately inoculated. *There are about eight tons of gunpowder in the colony.* To evince the great distress we are reduced to for want of bread, we must inform you

that we were obliged to buy thirty loaves of bread
of our baker to feed Colonel *De Haas'* detachment,
which entered this town *Friday* night, on their way
to join General *Arnold* at *La Chine*, and who could
not be supplied by the commissary. Such is our
extreme want of flour that we were yesterday
obliged to seize by force fifteen barrels to supply
this garrison with bread. Previous to this seizure a
general order was issued to the town-major to wait
on the merchants, or others having provisions or
merchandise for sale, requesting a delivery of what
our troops are in immediate want of, and requir-
ing him to give a receipt, expressing the quantity
delivered; for the payment of which the faith of
the United Colonies is pledged by your commissioners. Nothing but the most urgent necessity
can justify such harsh measures; but men with
arms in their hands will not starve when provisions can be obtained by force. To prevent a
general plunder, which might end in the massacre
of your troops, and of many of the inhabitants, we
have been constrained to advise the general to take
this step. We can not conceal our concern that
six thousand men should be ordered to *Canada*,
without taking care to have magazines formed for
their subsistence, cash to pay them, or to pay the
inhabitants for their labor, in transporting the baggage, stores, and provisions of the army. We can
not find words strong enough to describe our mis-

erable situation; you will have a faint idea of it if you figure to yourself an army broken and disheartened, half of it under inoculation, or under other diseases; soldiers without pay, without discipline, and altogether reduced to live from hand to mouth, depending on the scanty and precarious supplies of a few half-starved cattle, and trifling quantities of flour, which have hitherto been picked up in different parts of the country.

"Your soldiers grumble for their pay;—if they receive it they will not be benefited, as it will not procure them the necessaries they stand in need of. Your military chest contains but eleven thousand paper dollars. You are indebted to your troops treble that sum, and to the inhabitants above fifteen thousand dollars." [1]

*　　*　　*　　*　　*　　*　　*　　*　　*　　*

"SAMUEL CHASE,
　　CHARLES CARROLL *of Carrollton.*"

It would be difficult to draw a picture of more abject wretchedness than is given in this graphic letter of the commissioners, and it well prepares us for the consequences. Having done all in

---

[1] American Archives, vol. vi, pp. 589, 590.

their power to maintain our authority in Canada, Messrs. Chase and Carroll took their departure from Montreal on the 29th of May, to be present at a council of war of the general and field officers at Chamblay. On the 30th, it was resolved by this council to maintain possession of the strip of country "between the St. Lawrence and Sorel, *if possible*, and, in the meantime, to dispose matters *so as to make an orderly retreat out of Canada.*"[1]

On the 31st the commissioners passed from Chamblay to St. John's, where every thing was in confusion. On the morning of the 1st of June they found General Sullivan, who had arrived with fourteen hundred men during the night. Next day they took leave of the general, and sailed from St. John's on their journey homewards.

Thus ended the labors of the commissioners. They returned to Philadelphia, reported to congress, and congress voted to send new troops and to supply them properly.[2] But, in the meantime, the fate of our efforts in Canada was sealed. The last stand was made by General Sullivan. "Yet," says Mr. Sparks, "it was more resolute in purpose than successful in execution; the whole army was compelled precipitately to evac-

---

[1] See Carroll's Journal of those dates.
[2] See Journals of Congress for June, 1776, vol. ii, p. 206, ed. of 1800.

uate Canada, and retire over the lake to Crown Point.

"Montreal was held to the last moment. Arnold then drew off his detachment with no small risk of being intercepted by Sir Guy Carleton, and proceeded to St. John's, making, as General Sullivan wrote, 'a very prudent and judicious retreat, with an enemy close at his heels.' He had, two days before, been at St. John's, directed an encampment to be enclosed and ordered the frame of a vessel then on the stocks to be taken to pieces, the timbers numbered and the whole to be sent to Crown Point. General Sullivan soon arrived with the rear of his retreating army and preparations were made for an immediate embarkation. To this work Arnold applied himself with his usual activity and vigilance, remaining behind until he had seen every boat leave the shore but his own. He then mounted his horse, attended by Wilkinson, his aid-de-camp, and rode back two miles, when they discovered the enemy's advanced division in full march under General Burgoyne. They gazed at, or, in military phrase, reconnoitered it for a short time, and then hastened back to St. John's. A boat being in readiness to receive them, the horses were stripped and shot, the men were ordered on board, and Arnold, refusing all assistance, pushed off the boat with own hands; 'thus,' says Wilkinson, 'indulging the vanity of being the last man who embarked from the shores of the enemy.'"[1]

The commencement of this attack upon Canada was attended with brilliant success. The early efforts of Allen and Arnold at Ticonderoga and Crown Point are remarkable for daring courage. The career of Montgomery from the Isle Aux Noix to Quebec, and his storming of that stronghold, rank conspicuously among military exploits. The march of Arnold through the wilderness is characterized by dangers and hardships that would have appalled a less resolute soldier. And the siege of Quebec, with the shadow of an army, throughout a Canadian winter; the diplomacy of congress by its commissioners; and last, though not least, the honorable retreat of Sullivan and Arnold, hotly pursued as they were by Burgoyne to Sorel, Chamblay, and Isle Aux Noix,—all deserve to be remembered, by the student of this episode of our revolutionary struggles, as reflecting honor on the gallant men who retreated from those extremities of the British possessions to protect the vitals of the land in the approaching war of independence.

In this introductory sketch, the editor, to whom the Maryland Historical Society has confided so

---

[1] Sparks's Life of Arnold, p. 62.

pleasing a task, deems it useless to add a newly
written biography. The life of CHARLES CARROLL
OF CARROLLTON has been so frequently described,
that the people are familiar with it. Yet as the
writer who edited this work for the Maryland
Historical Society in 1845, and, thirty-one years
afterwards reperforms the task for the Centennial
Anniversary of our Nation in 1876,—possesses an
autograghic manuscript of Mr. Carroll setting forth
his biography for Mr. Delaplaine in 1816, it has
been thought fitting to preserve by printing such
a memorial of the survivor of all the patriots who
signed the Declaration of Independence. It will
be found in an appropriate place in this book,
together with an original letter, owned by the
Maryland Historical Society and now first published, written on the 2nd of June, 1776, to the
father of "the signer" by the Reverend John Carroll, immediately on his arrival in Philadelphia
from Canada.

The Diary which is now published was presented
by Mr. Carroll to his grand-daughter Mrs. Mac-
Tavish in 1823, and was deposited by her in 1844
among the archives of our society.

It is believed that this journal will be deeply
interesting to those who like to recur to the olden
times and to mark the improvement made in our
country within seventy years. The distance that
Mr. Carroll passed over in a month, may now

be accomplished with ease in a couple of days, whilst the wilderness he traversed has come to "blossom like a rose." [1] It is by no means the least memorable association with this valuable journal that its author was one of the fifty-six, who, soon afterwards signed the Declaration whose pledges produced so magical a change on the face of our country and on the welfare of mankind.

Baltimore, Maryland, 1 July, 1845, and May, 1876.

---

[1] In comparing the past with the present, it may not be uninteresting to record the fact that, in the year 1845, (when this Journal was first printed,) persons could travel from :

New York to Albany, 150 miles, by first class steamer, for .	. $	50
Albany to White Hall, by steamer and packet boat, 77 miles,	. 1	13
White Hall to St. John's by steamer, 150 miles, . . .	.	25
St. John's to La Prairie, by railway, 15 miles, . . .	.	50
La Prairie to Montreal, by steamer, 9 miles, ...	.	50

Time two days. In all, 401 miles, cost, ... $2 88

Painted by Vanloo.

Eng.d by H.B Hall.

BENJAMIN FRANKLIN.

JOURNAL

CHARLES CARROLL OF CARROLLTON,

DURING HIS

VISIT TO CANADA, IN 1776,

As one of the Commissioners from Congress.

PRIL 2d, 1776. Left New York at 5 o'clock, P. M.; sailed up North river, or Hudson's, that afternoon, about thirteen miles. About one o'clock in the night were awaked by the firing of cannon: heard three great guns distinctly from the Asia; soon saw a great fire, which we presumed to be a house on Bedloe's island, set on fire by a detachment of our troops. Intelligence had been received that the enemy were throwing up intrenchments on that island, and it had been determined by our generals to drive them

47

off. Dr. Franklin went upon deck, and saw waving flashes of light appearing suddenly and disappearing, which he conjectured to be the fire of musquetry, although he could not hear the report.

3d. A bad, rainy day; wind north-east; quite ahead. A. M., eleven o'clock, opposite to Colonel Phillips's (a tory); pretty situation near the river; garden sloping down to it; house has a pretty appearance; a church at a little distance on the south side, surrounded by cedar trees. The banks of the river, on the western side exceedingly steep and rocky; pine trees growing amidst the rocks. On the eastern, or New York side, the banks are not near so steep, they decline pretty gradually to the water's edge. The river is straight hitherto. About five o'clock wind breezed up from the south; got under way, and ran with a pretty easy gale as far as the highlands, forty miles from New York. The river here is greatly contracted, and the lands on each side very lofty. When we got into this strait the wind increased, and blew in violent flaws; in doubling one of these steep craggy points we were in danger of running on the rocks; endeavored to double the cape called St. Anthony's nose, but all our efforts proved ineffectual; obliged to return some way back in the straits to seek shelter; in doing this our mainsail was split to pieces by a sudden and most violent blast of wind off the mountains. Came to anchor: blew a perfect storm all night and all day the fourth. Remained all day (the fourth) in Thunder Hill bay, about half a mile below Cape St. Anthony's nose, and a quarter of a mile from Thunder Hill. Our crew were employed all this day in repairing the mainsail. The country round about this bay has a wild and romantic appearance; the hills are almost perpendicularly steep, and covered with rocks, and trees of a small size. The hill called St. Anthony's nose is said to be full of sulphur. I make no doubt this place has experienced some violent convulsion from subterraneous fire: the steepness of the hills, their correspondence, the narrowness of the river, and its depth, all confirm me in this opinion.

5th. Wind at north-east, mainsail not yet repaired. Sailed about twelve o'clock from Thunder Hill bay; just before we doubled Cape St. Anthony's nose, Mr. Chase and I landed to examine a beautiful fall of water. Mr. Chase, very apprehensive of the leg of mutton being boiled too much, impatient to get on board; wind breezing up, we had near a mile to row to overtake the vessel. As soon as we doubled Cape St. Anthony's nose a beautiful prospect opened on us. The river, from this place to Constitution fort, built on Marbler's rock, forms a fine canal, surrounded with high hills of various shapes; one, in particular, resembles a

7

sugar loaf, and is so called. About three miles from Cape St. Anthony's nose is another beautiful cascade, called "the Buttermilk." This is formed by a rivulet which flows from a lake on the top of a neighboring mountain; this lake, we were told, abounds with trout and perch. Arrived about five o'clock at Constitution fort; Mr. Chase went with me on shore to visit the fort; it is built on a rock called Marbler's rock: the river at this place makes a sudden bend to the west; the battery (for it does not deserve the name of a fort, being quite open on the north-east side) has two flanks, one fronting the south, and the other the west;—on the south flank were planted thirteen six and one nine pounder; on the west flank, seven nine pounders and one six pounder, but there were no cannoneers in the fort, and only one hundred and two men fit to do duty;—they intend to erect another battery on an eminence called Gravel hill, which will command vessels coming up the river as soon as they double Cape St. Anthony's nose. A little above this cape a battery is projected to annoy the enemy's vessels, to be called Fort Montgomery; they intend another battery lower down the river, and a little below Cape St. Anthony's nose. In the highlands are many convenient spots to construct batteries on; but, in order to make them answer the intended purpose, weighty metal should be placed on these batteries, and skilful

gunners should be engaged to serve the artillery.
About nine o'clock at night, the tide making, we
weighed anchor, and came to again about two
o'clock in the morning, the sixth instant. The
river is remarkably deep all the way through the
highlands, and the tide rapid. When we came
to an anchor off Constitution fort we found the
depth of water above thirty fathoms. These
highlands present a number of romantic views,
the steep hills overshadow the water, and in
some places the rocks, should they be rolled
down, would fall into the river several feet from
the banks on which they stood. This river seems
intended by nature to open a communication between Canada and the province of New York by
water, and, by some great convulsion, a passage
has been opened to the waters of Hudson's river
through the highlands. These are certainly a
spur of the Endless mountains.

6th. Weighed anchor about seven o'clock in the
morning: had a fine breeze; the country more
cultivated above the highlands; passed several
mills, all of them overshot; saw two frigates on
the stocks at Pokeepsay, building for the service
of the United Colonies; saw a great many lime-
kilns in our run this morning, on both sides
of the river, the banks of which begin to slope
more gradually to the water's edge. We wrote
to General Heath, from off Constitution fort, and

sent the letter to the commanding officer of the
fort, with orders to forward it by express immediately to the general at New York. The pur-
port of the letter was to inform the general of
the very defenceless condition of the fort, that
measures might be immediately taken to put it
in a better posture of defence. If Howe was a
man of enterprise, and knew of the weak state of
the fort, he might take it in its present situation
with sixty men, and without cannon. He might
land his party a little below the fort on the east
side, march over a marsh, and attack it on the
back part. It was proposed to erect a battery of
some cannon to sweep this marsh; but this, and
also the battery above mentioned, on Gravel hill,
have been strangely neglected, and nothing as yet
has been done towards constructing either of these
batteries, more than levelling the top of Gravel
hill.

Six o'clock, P. M., came to anchor four miles
from Albany; had a most glorious run this day,
and a most pleasant sail; including our run in
the night, we ran this day ninety-six miles—
Constitution fort being one hundred miles from
Albany, and sixty from New York. We passed
several country houses pleasantly situated on the
banks, or, rather, eminences commanding the
banks of the river; the grounds we could discover from the vessel did not appear to be

highly improved. We had a distant view of the
Katskill mountains. These are said to be some
of the highest in North America; they had a
pleasing appearance; the weather being somewhat hazy, they appeared like bluish clouds at
a great distance; when we were nearest to them,
they were distant about ten miles. Vast tracts
of land on each side of Hudson's river are held
by the proprietaries, or, as they are here styled,
the *Patrones* of manors. One of the Ransalaers
has a grant of twenty miles on each side of the
river. Mr. Robert R. Livingston informed me
that he held three hundred thousand acres. I
am told there are but ten original patentees between Albany and the highlands. The descendants of the first proprietaries of these immense
tracts still keep them in possession; necessity has
not as yet forced any of them to sell any part.

7th. Weighed anchor this morning about six
o'clock. Wind fair: having passed over the over-
slaw, had a distinct view of Albany, distant
about two miles:—landed at Albany at half past
seven o'clock; received, at landing, by GENERAL
SCHUYLER,[1] who, understanding we were coming
up, came from his house, about a mile out of

---

[1] Generel Philip Schuyler, who was one of our distinguished revolutionary soldiers, was born in 1733, at Albany. He entered the army
at the breaking out of the French war in 1755, and accompanied Sir
W. Johnson to Fort Edward and Lake George. After the peace of
1763, he undertook several civil employments. On the 25th of June,

town, to receive us and invite us to dine with him; he behaved with great civility; lives in pretty style; has two daughters (Betsy and Peggy), lively, agreeable, black eyed girls. Albany is situated partly on a level, and partly on the slope of a hill, or rising ground, on the west side of the river. Vessels drawing eight and nine feet water may come to Albany, and five miles even beyond it, at this season of the year, when the waters are out. The fort is in a ruinous condition, and not a single gun mounted on it. There are more houses in this town than in Annapolis, and I believe it to be much more populous. The citizens chiefly speak Dutch, being mostly the descendants of Dutchmen; but the English language and manners are getting ground apace.

9th. Left Albany early this morning, and travelled in a wagon in company with Mrs. Schuyler, her two daughters, and Generals Schuyler and

1775, (whilst a delegate to the Continental Congress,) he was appointed third major general of the American army; and was forthwith charged by Washington with the command of our forces in the province of New York. Here and in Canada he served the country with great ability, until the order was given to abandon that province. After this he displayed his patriotism and usefulness in various public employments of a a military character; and in April, 1779, congress, after his repeated solicitations, accepted the resignation of his command in the army. The benefit of his enlightened judgment and civil services was not denied to his country during the remainder of his life. His last few years were passed in dignified retirement; and, after suffering the most poignant anguish from the distressing fate of his beloved son-in-law, General Hamilton, he died at the age of seventy-one, on the 18th of November, 1804.

Thomas.   At six miles from Albany I quitted the
wagon and got on horse-back to accompany the
generals to view the falls on the Mohawk's river,
called the Cohooes.   The perpendicular fall is
seventy-four feet, and the breadth of the river at
this place, as measured by General Schuyler, is one
thousand feet.   The fall is considerably above one
hundred feet, taken from the first ripple or still
water above the perpendicular fall.   The river was
swollen with the melting of the snows and rains,
and rolled over the frightful precipice an impetu-
ous torrent.   The foam, the irregularities in the
fall broken by projecting rocks, and the deafening
noise, presented a sublime but terrifying spectacle.
At fifty yards from the place the water dropped
from the trees, as it does after a plentiful shower,
they being as wet with the ascending vapor as they
commonly are after a smart rain of some continu-
ance.   The bottoms adjoining the river Hudson
are fine lands, and appeared to be well cultivated;
most of them that we passed through were in
wheat, which, though commonly overflowed in the
spring, we were informed by our driver, suffered
no hurt, but were rather improved by the inun-
dation.   We arrived in the evening, a little before
sunset, at Saratoga, the seat of General Schuyler,
distant from Albany thirty-two miles.   We spent
the whole day in the journey, occasioned by the
badness of the roads, and the delay the wagons

met with in crossing two ferries.   The roads at this
season of the year are generally bad, but now worse
than ever, owing to the great number of wagons
employed in carrying the baggage of the regiments
marching into Canada, and supplies to the army
in that country.   General Schuyler informed me
that an uninterrupted water-carriage between New
York and Quebec might be perfected at fifty thousand pounds stirling expense, by means of locks,
and a small canal cut from a branch that runs
into Wood creek, and the head of a branch which
falls into Hudson's river; the distance is not more
than three miles.   The river Richelieu or Sorel, is
navigable for batteaux from the lake Champlain
into the St. Lawrence.   The rapids, below St.
John's, are not so considerable as to obstruct the
navigation of such vessels.

The lands about Saratoga are very good, particularly the bottom lands.   Hudson's river runs
within a quarter of a mile of the house, and you
have a pleasing view of it for two or three
miles above and below.   A stream called Fishkill,
which rises out of Lake Saratoga, about six miles
from the general's house, runs close by it, and
turns several mills; one, a grist mill, two saw
mills, (one of them carrying fourteen saws,) and
a hemp and flax mill.   This mill is a new construction, and answers equally well in breaking
hemp or flax.   I requested the general to get a

model made for me by the person who built it. Descriptions of machines are seldom accurately made, and when done with exactness are seldom understood. I was informed by the general that it is customary for the great proprietaries of lands to lease them out for three lives, sometimes on fee-farm-rents, reserving, by way of rent, a fourth, or, more commonly, a tenth of all the produce; but the proprietaries content themselves with a tenth of the wheat. On every transmutation of property from one tenant to another, a quarter part of what the land sells for is sometimes paid to the original proprietary or lord of the manor. The general observed to me that this was much the most advantageous way of leasing lands;—that in the course of a few years, from the frequent transmutations of tenants, the alienation fines would exceed the purchase of the fee-simple, though sold at a high valuation. General Schuyler is a man of a good understanding improved by reflection and study; he is of a very active turn, and fond of husbandry, and when the present distractions are composed, if his infirm state of health will permit him, will make Saratoga a most beautiful and most valuable estate. He saws up great quantities of plank at his mills, which, before this war, was disposed of in the neighborhood, but the greater part of it sent to Albany.

8

11th. Generals Thomas and Schuyler set off this morning for Lake George; the former to be in readiness to cross the lake on the first breaking up of the ice, the latter to forward the embarkation and transportation of military stores and supplies.

12th. It snowed all this morning until eleven o'clock; the snow above six inches deep on the ground: it was not off the neighboring hills when we left Saratoga.[1]

16th. This morning we set off from Saratoga; I parted with regret from the amiable family of General Schuyler; the ease and affability with which we were treated, and the lively behavior of the young ladies, made Saratoga a most pleasing *séjour*, the remembrance of which will long remain with me. We rode from Saratoga to McNeill's ferry, [distance two miles and a half,] crossed Hudson's river at this place, and rode on to one mile above Fort Miller, which is distant from McNeill's two miles. A Mr. Dover has a country-seat near Fort Miller; you see his house from the road. There is a very considerable fall in the river at Fort Miller. Just above it our

---

[1] Dr. Franklin addressed a friendly letter to Josiah Quincy, dated 15th of April, 1776, in which he says, "I am here on my way to Canada, detained by the present state of the lakes, in which the unthawed ice obstructs the navigation. I begin to apprehend that I have undertaken a fatigue that, at my time of life, may prove too much for me, *so I sit down to write to a few friends, by way of farewell.*"—See Sparks's Life of Franklin, vol. viii, p. 180.—*American Archives,* vol. v, p. 947.

baggage was put into another boat; it had been brought in a wagon from Saratoga to McNeill's, carried over the ferry in a wagon, and then put on board a boat, in which it was conveyed to the foot of Fort Miller falls; then carried over land a quarter of a mile and put into a second boat. At a mile from Fort Miller we got into a boat and went up the Hudson river to Fort Edward. Although this fort is but seven miles distant from the place where we took boat, we were above four hours rowing up. The current is exceedingly rapid, and the rapidity was increased by a freshet. In many places the current was so strong that the batteau men were obliged to set up with poles, and drag the boat by the painter. Although these fellows were active and expert at this business, it was with the greatest difficulty they could stem the current in particular places. The congress keeps in pay three companies of batteau men on Hudson's river, consisting each of thirty-three men with a captain;—the pay of the men is £4.10 per month. The lands bordering on Hudson's river, as you approach Fort Edward, become more sandy, and the principal wood that grows on them is pine. There are several saw mills both above and below Fort Miller. The planks sawed at the mills above Fort Miller are made up into small rafts and left without guides to the current of

the river; each one is marked, so that the raft-
men that remain just below Fort Miller falls,
watching for them coming down, may easily
know their own rafts. When they come over
the falls they go out in canoes and boats and
tow their rafts ashore, and then take them to
pieces and make them again into larger rafts.
The smaller rafts are called *cribs*. The ruins
only of Fort Edward remain; there is a good
large inn, where we found quartered Colonel Sinclair's regiment. Mr. Allen, son of old Mr.
Allen, is lieutenant-colonel; he received us very
politely and accommodated us with beds. The
officers of this regiment are in general fine sized
men, and seemed to be on a friendly footing;—
the soldiers also are stout fellows.

17th. Having breakfasted with Colonel Allen,
we set off from Fort Edward on our way to Fort
George. We had not got a mile from the fort
when a messenger from General Schuyler met
us. He was sent with a letter by the general to
inform us that Lake George was not open, and
to desire us to remain at an inn kept by one
Wing at seven miles distance from Fort Edward
and as many from Fort George. The country
between Wing's tavern and Fort Edward is very
sandy and somewhat hilly. The principal wood
is pine. At Fort Edward the river Hudson
makes a sudden turn to the westward; it soon

again resumes its former north course, for, at
a small distance, we found it on our left and
parallel with the road which we travelled, and
which, from Fort Edward to Fort George, lies
nearly north and south. At three miles, or
thereabouts, from Fort Edward, is a remarkable
fall in the river. We could see it from the
road, but not so as to form any judgment of its
height. We were informed that it was upwards
of thirty feet, and is called the Kingsbury falls.
We could distinctly see the spray arising like a
vapor or fog from the violence of the fall. The
banks of the river, above and below these falls
for a mile or two, are remarkably steep and
high, and appear to be formed or faced, with a
kind of stone very much resembling slate. The
banks of the Mohawk's river at the Cohooes are
faced with the same sort of stone;—it is said to
be an indication of sea-coal. Mr. Wing's tavern
is in the township of Queensbury, and Charlotte
county; Hudson's river is not above a quarter of
a mile from his house. There is a most beautiful fall in the river at this place. From still
water, to the foot of the fall, I imagine the fall
cannot be less than sixty feet, but the fall is not
perpendicular; it may be about a hundred and
twenty or a hundred and fifty feet long, and in
this length, it is broken into three distinct falls,
one of which may be twenty-five feet nearly

perpendicular. I saw Mr. Wing's patent,—the reserved quit-rent is two shillings and sixpence sterling per hundred acres; but he informs me it has never been yet collected.

18th. We set off from Wing's tavern about twelve o'clock this day, and reached Fort George [1] about two o'clock; the distance is eight miles and a half;—you can not discover the lake until you come to the heights surrounding it,—the descent from which to the lake is nearly a mile long;— from these heights you have a beautiful view of the lake for fifteen miles down it. Its greatest breadth during these fifteen miles does not exceed a mile and a quarter, to judge by the eye, which, however, is a very fallacious way of estimating distances. Several rocky islands appear in the lake, covered with a species of cedar called here *hemlock*. Fort George is in as ruinous a condition as Fort Edward, it is a small bastion, faced with stone, and built on an eminence command- ing the head of the lake. There are some barracks

[1] See General Schuyler's letter to Washington, dated Fort George, April 27, 1776, *Am. Archives*, vol. v, p. 1097; and the letter immedi- ately following, from Arnold to Schuyler, dated at Montreal on the 20th April. These letters give gloomy views of Canadian affairs. The reader will not be amazed, after reading Arnold's account of our army and its resources, that it finally retreated from the province.

According to Arnold's returns of the troops before Quebec on the 30th March, 786 were on the sick list out of 2505, most of whom were griev- ously ill of the small-pox.—"Fifteen hundred of these men," he says, "are at liberty on the 15th of April, and probably not more than half of them will be retained in the service."

in it, in which the troops were quartered, or rather
one barrack, which occupied almost the whole space
between the walls. At a little distance from this
fort, and to the westward of it, is the spot where
the Baron Dieskau was defeated by Sir William
Johnson.[1] About a quarter of a mile further to
the westward the small remains of Fort William
Henry are to be seen across a little rivulet which

---

[1] See Chalmers's History of the Revolt of the American Colonies, vol.
ii, p. 277, and Smith's History of New York, vol. ii, p. 220.

The Baron Dieskau had collected about 3000 men at Crown Point,
and led a detachment of 200 regulars, 600 Canadians, and as many
Indians, up the South bay, intending to pass on and lay waste the set-
tlements down to Albany; but, near Fort Edward, he turned back, with
hopes of cutting off that part of the army which was then fourteen miles
higher up the lake. He was first met by a party of about 1000 men,
a few miles from our camp. He drove them before him, as well as a
detachment sent to support them; but, by a very great error, instead of
storming the log breastwork, he halted and scattered his irregulars at
one hundred and fifty yards, keeping up a fire of *musquetry*, until the
camp recovered from its surprise and began to play upon them with
artillery.

Wounded, and deserted by all but his handful of regulars, he endeavored to reach his boats at South bay; but was pursued, wounded again,
and taken. A detachment of 200 men from Fort Edward, arriving at
this instant, pursued the flying army, and completed the repulse before
the dusk of evening. Sir William Johnson received a wound in the
thigh early in the action, and the defence was conducted by General
Lyman.

Dieskau had been a favorite soldier of Saxe, and by his recommendation had been entrusted by the French government with command in
Canada. He was long retained a prisoner in England, and, I believe,
died there from the effects of the wounds received in this fatal action.
His account of the battle and his correspondence with his government
may be seen in the collection of MSS. lately made by Mr. Brodhead for
the state of New York, and deposited at Albany in the Secretary of
State's office.—See vol. xi of the *Paris Documents*, pp. 117, 123, 125.

In February, 1756, parliament granted at the request of the colonies,
whose troops had defeated Dieskau, £115,000, not so much as a reim-
bursement as a bounty; more as an encouragement for future exploits,
than as a reward for the past.

forms a swamp, and is the morass mentioned by
Sir William Johnson in his account of the action
with Dieskau.   Fort William Henry was taken
last war by Montcalm and destroyed;—the garrison, consisting of four hundred men, and sixteen
hundred others that were intrenched without the
fort, capitulated; — a considerable part of these
men were murdered by the Indians, on their
march to Fort Edward, after they had delivered
up their arms, according to the terms of capitulation.   The bay in which Montcalm landed is
seen from Fort George; he left a guard of five
hundred men only to protect his boats and artillery, and marched round over the heights to
come to the southward of Fort William Henry.
When on these heights, he discovered the intrenched body without the fort, and seeing the
great indiscretion he had been guilty of in leaving so small a force to guard his baggage and
boats, he rashly marched back to secure them.
Had our troops attacked Montcalm's five hundred men, they would probably have defeated
them, taken his cannon and boats, and forced
him to surrender with his whole army.   There was
nothing to impede the attack but want of enterprise and conduct in the commanding officer. [1]

[1] See Smith's History of New York, vol. ii, pp. 245–6, and Chalmers's
History of the Revolt of the American Colonies, vol. ii, pp. 287–8.
  " Montcalm, who succeeded Dieskau in command, crossed Lake Cham-
plain with eleven thousand men, and a numerous artillery, and invested

The neighborhood of Fort George abounds with limestone, and so indeed does all the country surrounding the lake, and all the islands in it. Their rocky coast and bottom contribute, no doubt, to the clearness of the lake water. Never did I see water more transparent, and to its transparency, no doubt, must be ascribed the excellency of the fish in this lake, which much exceed the fish in Lake Champlain. Lake George abounds with perch, trout, rock, and eels.

19th. We embarked at Fort George this evening, about one o'clock, in company with General Schuyler, and landed in Montcalm's bay about four miles from Fort George. After drinking tea on shore, and arranging matters in our boats, we again embarked, and went about three or four miles further, then landed, (the sun being set,) and kindled fires on shore. The longest of the boats, made for the transportation of the troops over lakes George and Champlain, are

---

Fort William Henry in the beginning of August, 1757. This fort had been erected subsequently to the Crown Point expedition. Webb, who lay in its vicinity at Fort Edward, with four thousand regulars and provincials, did every thing for its relief that could be expected from an intelligent officer. But he found it impossible to collect the numerous militias of the neighboring provinces, since they never had been embodied under any system, and the authority of the governors had long been sacrificed to the passions of the multitude.

"Monro defended Fort William Henry with a gallantry that gained him the applause of his conquerer, who could not, however, protect a brave garrison from the plunder of the savages. Montcalm, after this, retired into Canada, and so ended the third campaign of that war."

thirty-six feet in length and eight feet wide; they draw about a foot water when loaded, and carry between thirty and forty men, and are rowed by the soldiers. They have a mast fixed in them, to which a square sail, or a blanket is fastened, but these sails are of no use unless with the wind abaft or nearly so. After we left Montcalm bay we were delayed considerably in getting through the ice; but, with the help of tentpoles, we opened ourselves a passage through it into free water. The boats fitted up to carry us across had awnings over them, under which we made up our beds, and my fellow travellers slept very comfortably; but this was not my case, for I was indisposed the whole night, with a violent sickness at my stomach and vomiting, occasioned by an indigestion. We left the place where we passed the night very early on the 20th.

20th. We had gone some miles before I rose; soon after I got out of bed we found ourselves entangled in the ice. We attempted, but in vain, to break through it in one place, but were obliged to desist and force our passage through another, which we effected without much difficulty. At eight o'clock we landed to breakfast. After breakfast the general looked to his small boat; being desirous to reach the landing at the north end of Lake George, we set off

together; but the general's boat and the other
boat, with part of the luggage, soon got before us
a considerable way. After separating, we luckily
fell in with the boat bringing the Montreal and
Canada mail, by which we were informed that
the west shore of the lake, at a place called
Sabatay point, was much encumbered with ice,
but that there was a free passage on the east
side; accordingly, we kept along the east shore,
and found it free from ice, by which means we
got before the general and the other boat; for
the general, who was foremost, had been delayed
above an hour in breaking through the ice, and,
in one place, was obliged to haul his boat over
a piece or neck of land thirty feet broad. Dr.
Franklin found in the Canada mail, which he
opened, a letter for General Schuyler. When we
had weathered Sabatay point, we stood over for
the western shore of the lake, and a mile or two
below the point we were overtaken by the general, from whom we learned the cause of his delay.
Mr. Chase and myself went on board the general's
boat, and reached the landing place at the south
end of Lake George near two hours before the
other boats. Lake George lies nearly north and
south, or rather, as I think, somewhat to the
eastward of a due north course. Its shores are
remarkably steep, high, and rocky (particularly
the east shore), and are covered with pine and

cedar, or what is here termed hemlock; the country is wild, and appears utterly incapable of cultivation; it is a fine deer country, and likely to
remain so, for I think it never will be inhabited.
I speak of the shores, and I am told the inland
country resembles these. The lake, in its greatest width, does not exceed, I think, two miles;
the widest part is nearest the north end, immediately before you enter the last narrows, which
are not, in their greatest width, above half a
mile. There are two places where the lake is
considerably contracted, one about the middle of
it, the other, as I have said, at the north end;
this last gradually contracts itself in breadth to
the size of an inconsiderable river, and suddenly,
in depth, to that of a very shallow one. The
landing place of Lake George is a few yards to
the southward of the first fall or ripple in this
river, through which the waters of Lake George
drain into Lake Champlain. We passed through
this ripple, and though our boat did not draw
above seven or eight inches, her bottom raked
the rocks; the water ran through this passage
about as swift as it does through your tail race.
From the landing place to Ticonderoga is three
miles and a half. The boats, in coming through
Lake George, pass through the passage just described, and unload at a quarter of a mile below
the usual landing place. Their contents are then

put into wagons, and carried over to Ticonderoga.
General Schuyler has erected a machine for rais-
ing the boats when emptied, and then letting
them gently down on a carriage constructed for
the purpose, on which they are drawn over land
to Ticonderoga, on Lake Champlain, to carry the
troops over the last mentioned lake, and down
the Sorel into the river St. Lawrence. These
carriages consist of four wheels, united by a long
sapling, at the extremities of which the wheels
are placed; over the axletrees is fixed a piece
of wood, on which each end of the boat is supported and made fast by a rope secured round a
bolt at the undermost part, and in the centre of
the axletree. This bolt is made of iron, and
passes through the aforesaid pieces of wood and
the axletree. These carriages are drawn by six
oxen, and this morning (21st instant) I saw three
or four boats carried over upon them. Lake
George, from the south end of it to the landing
place at the north extremity, is thirty-six miles
long. Its average width does not, I think, exceed a mile, and this breadth is interspersed and
broken by innumerable little rocky islands formed
of limestone; the shores of which are commonly
so steep that you may step from the rocks into
ten or twelve feet water. The season was not
sufficiently advanced to admit of catching fish, a
circumstance we had reason to regret, as they are

so highly praised by the connoisseurs in good eat-
ing, and as one of our company is so excellent a
judge in this science. There are no considerable
rivers that empty themselves into Lake George.
We saw some brooks or rivulets, which, I pre-
sume, after the melting of the snows, are almost
dry. The lake must be fed, principally, with
springs, the melting of snows, and the torrents
that must pour into it, from its high and steep
shores, after rains. As there is no considerable
river that flows into it, so is the vent of its
waters into Lake Champlain very inconsiderable.
In summer you may step, dry-footed, from rock
to rock, in the place which I have called the
first ripple, and which I said we passed, coming
out of Lake George. The water suddenly shal-
lows from a great depth to nine or ten feet or
less. This change is immediately discoverable by
the great change in the color of the water. The
lake water is of a dark bluish cast, and the water
of the river of a whitish color, owing not only to
the difference of the depth, but the difference of
the bottoms and shores, which, adjoining the river,
are of white clay.

21st. I took a walk this evening to the saw-
mill which is built on the principal fall of the
river flowing from Lake George into Lake Champlain. At the foot of this fall, which is about
thirteen feet high, the river is navigable for bat-

teaux into Lake Champlain. From the saw-mill to the place where the batteaux are put on carriages to be carried over land, the distance is one mile and a half. I saw them unload a boat from the carriage, and launch it, at the same time, into the river; this was performed by thirty-five or forty men. To-day they carried over this portage fifty batteaux. I saw the forty-eighth put on the carriage. A little to the north-westward of the saw-mill, on the west side of the river, I visited the spot where Lord Howe was killed. At a small expense a continued navigation for batteaux might be made between the lakes George and Champlain, by means of a few locks. General Schuyler informed me that locks, sufficient and adequate to the above purpose, might be constructed for fifteen hundred pounds sterling. There are but four or five falls in this river, the greatest of which is not above fourteen or fifteen feet. But the general informs me a much more advantageous water carriage may be opened through Wood creek, which falls into Lake Champlain at Skeenesborough, twenty-eight miles south of Ticonderoga. The general proposes to have this creek accurately surveyed, the heights ascertained, and estimate made of the expense of erecting locks on Wood creek, and the most convenient branch which heads near it and falls into Hudson's river. If this water

communication between Lake Champlain and the
province of New York should be perfected, there
is little danger of the enemy's gaining the mastery of Lake Champlain, or of their ever having
it in their power to invade these colonies from
Canada with any prospect of success, besides the
security which will be obtained for the colonies in
time of war by making this navigation.   Trade,
during peace, will be greatly benefited by it, as
there will then be a continued water communication between New York and Canada, without the
inconvenience and expense attending the portages
over land.

22d. I this morning took a ride with General
Schuyler across the portage, or from the landing
place at the bottom of Lake George, to Ticonderoga.   The landing place is properly on the river
which runs out of Lake George into Lake Champlain, and may be a mile and a half from the
place where the former may be said to terminate,
i. e., where the lake is contracted into a river, as
a current and shallow water.   This river, comput-
ing its length from the aforesaid spot to the foot
of the falls at the saw-mills, and its windings,
which are inconsiderable, is not more than four
or five miles long.   From the foot of the saw-
mill falls there is still water into Lake Champlain.   It is at the foot of these falls that the
batteaux, brought over land, are launched into

the water, and the artillery and the apparatus belonging to it are embarked in them; the stores, such as provisions, ball, powder, &c., are embarked from Ticonderoga. At sixty or seventy yards below the saw-mill there is a bridge built over the river:—this bridge was built by the king during the last war;—the road from the landing place to Ticonderoga passes over it, and you then have the river on the right; when you have passed the bridge you immediately ascend a pretty high hill, and keep ascending till you reach the famous lines made by the French in the last war, which Abercrombie was so infatuated as to attack with musquetry only; —his cannon was lying at the bridge, about a mile or something better from these lines. The event of the day is too well known to be mentioned; we lost [killed and wounded] near one thousand six hundred men; had the cannon been brought up, the French would not have waited to be attacked;—it was morally impossible to succeed against these lines with small arms only, particularly in the manner they were attacked; —our army passing before them, and receiving a fire from the whole extent;—whereas, had it marched lower down, or to the north-west of these lines, it would have flanked them:—they were constructed of large trunks of trees, felled on each other, with earth thrown up against

10

them. On the side next the French troops, they had, besides felling trees, lopped and sharpened their branches, and turned them towards the enemy; the trunks of the trees remain to this day piled up as described, but are fast going to decay. As soon as you enter these lines you have a full view of Lake Champlain and Ticonderoga fort, distant about a quarter of a mile. The land from thence gradually declines to the spot on which the fort is built.[1] Lake Champlain empties itself opposite the fort, and runs south twenty-eight miles to Skeenesborough. Crown Point is fifteen miles down the lake from Ticonderoga. The lake is no where broad in sight of the last mentioned place, but the

[1] The works at Ticonderoga were trifling; logs had been piled up on the land side in a line for a breastwork, with trees before it to embarrass assailants. In August, 1758, Abercrombie, who was not informed that there was, at one end, an open access to the French encampment, ordered an attack with *musquetry* alone, upon that part of the line which was completed and fortified with cannon. It was at that point that the British sustained a loss of nearly two thousand men in killed and wounded.

The French general, who was just within the lines, perceived the folly of the British in advancing through the obstructions of an *abattis* of trees, and forbade a musket to be fired until he gave the word. As soon as the English troops were so completely within his toils that their embarrassments utterly impeded flight, he issued the word of command, and the assailants were slaughtered like cattle.

It was related by Colonel Schuyler, who was then a prisoner in Canada, that Montcalm's whole force at Crown Point did not exceed three thousand men, nor his killed, wounded, and captured, two hundred and thirty. From a dread of the British superiority, he had actually resolved, before Abercrombie retreated, to abandon Crown Point.— See *Smith's History of New York*, vol. ii, p. 265.

prospect from it is very pleasing; its shores are not as steep as those of Lake George. They rise gradually from the water, and are covered more thickly with woods, which grow in good soils, or at least in soils much better than can be seen on Lake George. There is but one settlement on the latter, at Sabatay point; I understood there were about sixty acres of good land at that point. Ticonderoga fort is in a ruinous condition; it was once a tolerable fortification. The ramparts are faced with stone. I saw a few pieces of cannon mounted on one bastion, more for show, I apprehend, than service. In the present state of affairs this fort is of no other use than as an *entrepôt* or magazine for stores, as from this place all supplies for our army in Canada are shipped to go down Lake Champlain. I saw four vessels, viz: three schooners and one sloop; these are to be armed, to keep the mastery of the lake in case we should lose St. John's and be driven out of Canada;—in the meantime they will be employed in carrying supplies to our troops in that country. Of these three schooners, two were taken from the enemy on the surrender of St. John's, one of them is called the Royal Savage, and is pierced for twelve guns; she had, when taken, twelve brass pieces — I think four and six pounders; these were sent to Boston. She is really a fine vessel, and built on purpose for fighting; however, some repairs are wanted; a new mainmast must be put in, her old one being shattered with one of our cannon balls.[1] When these vessels are completely rigged, armed and manned, we may defy the enemy on Lake Champlain for this summer and fall at least, even should we unfortunately be driven out of Canada. When our small army last summer, or rather fall, [in number about one thousand

---

[1] This vessel had been taken the year before. After Ticonderoga and Crown Point were secured by Colonel Allen, a party of his troops came suddenly upon Major Skeene, at Skeenesborough, and, making him prisoner, also seized a schooner and several batteaux, with which they hastened to Ticonderoga. Allen and Arnold then formed a plan to make a rapid descent upon St. John's, take a king's sloop that lay there, and attempt a descent upon the garrison. The schooner and batteaux were therefore speedily manned and armed, and, as Arnold had been a seaman in his youth, the schooner was assigned to his command, while the batteaux were committed to the charge of Allen. They left Ticonderoga at nearly the same time; but, as the wind was fresh, the schooner outsailed the batteaux. At eight o'clock in the evening of the 17th May, 1775, Arnold was within thirty miles of St. John's; and, as the weather was calm, he fitted out two batteaux with thirty-five men, leaving the schooner behind, and proceeded to his destination, where he arrived at six o'clock next morning. He immediately made his attack, seized a sergeant with twelve men, and the king's sloop of about seventy tons, with two brass sixes, and seven men. Neither side sustained any loss; and embarking, after a delay of two hours, he took with him his captives, the sloop, and four batteaux, having destroyed five others.

Fifteen miles from St John's he met Allen pressing forward with his party. They saluted in honor of the victory, and the colonel pushed on with one hundred men towards *La Prairie*, to keep, if possible, the ground that had been taken by Arnold. But, notwithstanding his resolution and courage, he was soon obliged to retreat before reinforcements that came from Chamblay and elsewhere, and he returned to Ticonderoga, with a loss of only three men, who had been taken prisoners.—See *Sparks's American Biography*, vol. i, p. 279, et seq.

seven hundred,] came to *Isle aux Noix*, this vessel was almost ready to put to sea, she wanted only as much to be done to her as could easily have been finished in three days, had the enemy exerted themselves. Had she ventured out our expedition to Canada must have failed, and probably our whole army must have surrendered, for she was greatly an overmatch for all the naval strength we then had on the lake. Had Preston, who commanded at St. John's, ventured out with his garrison, consisting of six hundred men, and attacked our people at their first landing, he would, in all probability, have defeated them, as they were a mere undisciplined rabble, made up chiefly of the offings and outcasts of New York.

23d. We continued this day at the landing place, our boats not being yet ready and fitted to carry us through Lake Champlain. General Schuyler and the troops were busily engaged in carting over land, to the saw-mill, the batteaux, cannon, artillery stores, provisions, &c., there to be embarked on the navigable waters of Lake Champlain, and transported over that lake to St. John's.

24th. We this day left the landing place at Lake George and took boat at the saw-mill. From the saw-mill to Ticonderoga, the distance, by water, is about a mile; the water is shallow, but sufficiently deep for batteau navigation. A little below the bridge before mentioned, the French, during the last war, drove pickets into the river, to prevent our boats getting round from the saw-mill to Ticonderoga with the artillery; some of the pickets still remain, for both our boats struck on them. Ticonderoga fort[1] is beautifully situated, but, as I said before, it is in a ruinous condition;—neither is the place, in my opinion, judiciously chosen for the construction of a fort; a fort constructed at the saw-mill would much better secure the passage or pass into the province of New York by way of Lake George. Having waited at Ticonderoga an hour or two, to take in provisions for the crews of both boats, consisting entirely of soldiers, we embarked at eleven o'clock, and reached Crown Point a little after three, with the help of our oars only. Crown Point is distant from Ticonderoga only fifteen miles. The lake, all the way, from one part to another, is narrow, scarce exceeding a mile on an average. Crown Point is situated on a neck or isthmus of land, on the west side of the lake; it is in ruins; it was once a considerable fortress, and the English must have expended a large sum in

---

[1] For an interesting account of the capture of this place by Ethan Allen, on the morning of the 10th of May, 1775, "*In the name*," as he said, "*of the Great Jehovah and the Continental Congress;*" see *Sparks's American Biography, first series*, vol. i, p. 274, et seq.

constructing the fort and erecting the barracks, which are also in ruins. A great part of the ditch is cut out of the solid limestone rock. This ditch was made by blowing the rocks, as the holes bored for the gunpowder are plainly to be seen in the fragments. By some accident the fort took fire, the flames communicated to the powder magazine, containing at that time ninety-six barrels. The shock was so great as to throw down the barracks—at least the upper stories. The explosion was distinctly heard ten miles off, and the earth shook at that distance as if there had been an earthquake. This intelligence I received from one Faris, who lives ten miles down the lake, and at whose house we lay this night. The wood-work of the barracks is entirely consumed by fire, but the stone work of the first stories might be easily repaired, and one of these barracks might be converted into a fine manufactory. The erecting of these barracks and the fort must have cost the government not less, I dare say, than one hundred thousand pounds sterling.[1] The lake is narrow opposite

---

[1] As soon as Ethan Allen had got possession of Ticonderoga and secured his prisoners, he dispatched Seth Warner with a detachment of men to seize Crown Point. The distance was only fifteen miles, but a strong head wind drove back the boats, and the whole party returned the same evening. A day or two afterwards, however, the attempt was successfully renewed. The garrison—consisting of eleven men and a sergeant—was captured, and sixty-one good cannon, and fifty-three unfit for service, were taken.—See *Sparks's American Biography*, vol. i, p. 277.

the fort, and makes a bend, by which the
vessels passing on the lake were much exposed
to the artillery of the fort; and this advantageous situation first induced the French, and
then the English, to erect a fort here. The
French fort was inconsiderable, and close to
the water; the English fort is a much more
extensive fortification, and farther from the lake,
but so as to command it.

25th. We set off from Faris's at five o'clock
in the morning. If Faris's information may be
relied on, his land and the neighboring lands
are exceedingly fine;—he told us he had reaped
thirty bushels of wheat from the acre; the soil
appears to be good; but, to judge of it from
its appearance, I should not think it so fertile.
Three miles north of Faris's the lake begins to
contract itself, and this contraction continues for
six miles, and is called the narrows. At Faris's
the lake is about two miles wide. We breakfasted in a small cove at a little distance to the
southward of the Split rock. The Split rock is
nine miles from Faris's house. At the Split
rock the lake grows immediately wider as you
go down it; its width, in this place, can not be
much short of seven miles. When we had got
four or five miles from the rock, the wind headed
us, and blew a fresh gale, which occasioned a
considerable swell on the lake, the wind being

northeast, and having a reach of twenty miles. We were constrained to put in at one McCaully's, where we dined on cold provisions. The wind abating about four o'clock, we put off again and rowed seven miles down the lake to a point of land a mile or two to the southward of four islands called the Four Brothers; these islands lie nearly in the middle of the lake, which is very wide in this place, and continues so far as you can see down it. Mr. Chase and I slept this night on shore under a tent made of bushes.

26th.[1] We set off this morning at four o'clock from the last mentioned point, which I called "Commissioners' point." Wind fair; a pretty breeze. At five o'clock reached Schuyler's island; it contains eight hundred acres, and belongs to Montreson, distant seven miles from the Four Brothers. Schuyler's island lies near the western shore. The lake continues wide; at ten o'clock got to Cumberland head, fourteen miles from Schuyler's island. Cumberland head is the south point of Cumberland bay. The bay forms a deep recess on the western side of the lake; its length, from Schuyler's island, at the point of land opposite to it, to Cumberland head-land, is fourteen

---

[1] On the 26th of April, 1776, the President of Congress addressed letters to the commissioners, and to General Schuyler, upon the subject of the late disturbances in Canada.—See *Am. Arch.*, vol. v, pp. 1085, 1086. For the *resolutions* spoken of, see *same volume*, p. 1686.

miles, and its depth not less than nine or ten
miles. The wind luckily favored us until we
reached Cumberland head; it then ceased;—it
grew cloudy, and soon began to rain, and the
wind shifted to the north-east. We breakfasted
at Cumberland head on tea and good biscuit, our
usual breakfast, having provided ourselves with
the necessary furniture for such a breakfast. As
soon as it cleared up we rowed across a bay,
about four miles wide, to *Point aux Roches*, so
called from the rocks of which it is formed.
Indeed it is one entire stone wall, fifteen feet
high, but gradually inclining to the north-east.
At that extremity it is little above the water.
Having made a short stay at this place to
refresh our men, we rowed round the point,
hugged the western shore, and got into a cove
which forms a very safe harbor. But the ground
being low and swampy, and no cedar or hemlock
trees, of the branches of which our men formed
their tents at night, we thought proper to cross
over to *Isle la Motte*, bearing from us about
north-east, and distant three miles. The island
is nine miles long and one broad. The south-
west side of it is high land, and the water is
deep close in shore, which is rocky and steep.
We lay under this shore all night in a critical
situation, for had the wind blown hard in the
night, from the west, our boats would probably

have been stove against the rocks. We passed
the night on board the boats, under the awning
which had been fitted up for us. This awning
could effectually secure us from the wind and
rain, and there was space enough under it to
make up four beds. The beds we were provi-
dent enough to take with us from Philadelphia.
We found them not only convenient and com-
fortable, but necessary; for, without this precau-
tion, persons travelling from the colonies into
Canada at this season of the year, or indeed at
any other, will find themselves obliged either to
sit up all night, or to lie on the bare ground or
planks. Several of the islands in Lake Champlain have different claimants, as patents have
been granted by the French government and the
government of New York. According to the
present division, most of them, indeed all, except
Isle aux Noix, are in the colony of New York.

27th. A fine morning. We left our nation's
station at four o'clock, and rowed ten miles to
Point au Fer, so called from some iron mines
at no great distance from it; the land here, and
all the adjacent country, is very flat and low.
Colonel Christie has built a house at this point,
which is intended for a tavern; the place is
judiciously chosen. A small current begins here,
and the raftsmen are not obliged to row; after
they bring their rafts to *Point au Fer*, the

current will carry them in a day to St. John's,
which is distant from this point thirty measured
miles. Windmill point is three miles below
Point au Fer; and, a mile or two below the
former, runs the line which divides the province
of Quebec from New York. At Windmill point
the lake begins to contract itself to the size of
a river, but of a large and deep one. Opposite
to this point the width can not be much short
of two miles: six miles below Windmill point
you meet with a small island called *Isle aux
Têtes:* from a number of heads that were stuck
upon poles by the Indians after a great battle
that was fought between them on this island,
or near it. At this island the current is not
only perceptible, but strong. We went close by
the island, and in shallow water, which gave us
a better opportunity of observing the switfness of
the current. A mile or two below this island,
we breakfasted at a tavern kept by one Stodd.
At *Isle aux Têtes*, the river *Richelieu*, or St.
John's, or Sorel (for it goes by all these names),
may be properly said to begin. It is in this
place above a mile wide, deep, and the current
considerable;—its banks are almost level with
the water,—indeed, the water appears to be
rather above the banks; the country is one
continued swamp, overflowed by the river at
this season; as you approach St. John's the

current grows stronger. *Isle aux Noix* is half way between St. John's and *Point au Fer*, and consequently fifteen miles from each; we passed close by it: it is very level and low, covered at the north end with hazel bushes; but the land is higher than the banks of the river.[1] We saw the intrenchments thrown up by the French during the last war, and the remains of the pickets driven into the river, quite across to the island, to prevent the English boats from

[1] In a letter from Colonel Ethan Allen to congress, on the 2d June, 1776, he speaks of his expedition as one undertaken at the special encouragement and request of a number of gentlemen in the colony of Connecticut. After alluding to his successes, he declares that the key of Canada is yet ours, and strongly recommends that two or three thousand men should be pushed into that province, so as to weaken General Gage, and insure us the country. He even believed that if he could be thus furnished, he would find it no insuperable difficulty to take Quebec.

If, however, it was thought premature to push an army into Canada, he proposed to make a stand at the Isle aux Noix, which had been fortified by the intrenchments of the French during the last war, and had greatly fatigued our large army to take it.

Allen's advice was deemed bold and incautious when given, but events afterwards proved that it was characterized by wisdom and forethought. If a competent force had been thrown into Canada before the British had time to rally their scattered forces, the campaign would have rewarded us with success instead of the sad failure that attended the wavering and tardy policy pursued by congress in maturing the expedition.

Congress, or the country had, however, at this moment, not yet resolved how far they would enlist the Canadians in the enterprise, and could not but have regarded the attack on their French neighbors as very much like a distinct war from that undertaken against the British. The first effort of the colonies was to secure their own immediate possessions; the next, to prevent injury to them from such possessions as Great Britain might retain. The reader will observe that Mr. Carroll fully agreed with Colonel Allen as to the great importance of this military position at the Isle aux Noix.—See *Sparks's Am. Biog*, vol. 1, p. 283 *et seq.*, *et* p. 287.

getting down to St. John's. These fortifications induced Gen'l Amherst to penetrate into Canada by Oswego lake and the St. Lawrence, rather than run the hazard of being stopped at *Isle aux Noix*. Indeed I believe he would have found it a difficult matter to force his way through this pass, which appears to me of great consequence in the present contest, should the forces of the United Colonies be obliged to evacuate Canada; for if we occupy and fortify this island, drive pickets into the river, and build row galleys, and place them behind the pickets, or between the little islets formed by the several smaller islands, almost contiguous to *Isle aux Noix*, the enemy will not be able to penetrate into the colonies from Canada by the way of Lake Champlain. It is certain that Amherst, rather than expose himself to the disgrace of being foiled at this post, chose to make a roundabout march of several hundred leagues, and encounter the rapids of the St. Lawrence, by which he lost some of his boats and several hundred men.[1]   Having

[1] General Amherst left Schenectady in June, 1760, to join an army of four thousand regulars and six thousand provincials, who were to descend into the heart of the French colony by the St. Lawrence. Meanwhile General Murray was to approach, with two thousand regulars, from Quebec, whilst five thousand provincials, under Colonel Haviland, were to penetrate by Lake Champlain. Sir William Johnson also held out a promise of assistance by a large body of Indian allies, of whom not more than six hundred accompanied the western army for a short distance, and then returned to their villages and hunting grounds.

The three grand divisions, however, met in the neighborhood of

passed the *Isle aux Noix*, the wind sprang up in
our favor;—assisted by the wind and current, we
reached St. John's at three o'clock. Before I
speak of this fortress, it may not be improper to
make some remarks on the navigation of Lake
Champlain, the adjacent country, and its appearance. The navigation appears to be very secure,
as there are many inlets, coves, and harbors, in
which such vessels as will be used on the lake
may at all times find shelter; the water is deep,
at least wherever we touched, close in with the
land. There are several islands in the lake, the
most considerable of which we saw; the principal
is *Grand isle*,—it deserves the appellation, being,
as we were informed, twenty-seven miles long,
and three or four miles wide. *Isle la Motte* is
the next largest, and *Isle de Belle Cour* ranks
after that. *Isle la Motte* we touched at; the
others we could plainly distinguish. We saw
several of the islands on the eastern shore of
the lake, some of which appear as large as Pop-
lar's island; but having no person on board our
boats acquainted with the lake, we could not

Montreal, and drove the enemy's forces into the island, when, being
surrounded and unable to resist, Monsieur Vaudrieul, the governor,
surrendered all Canada to the British on the 8th of September. It was
whilst Amherst was proceeding north, on this expedition, that he was
forced to avoid the French at Isle aux Noix, and thus lost some valuable troops in the perilous navigation of the St. Lawrence. This result
confirms Allen's view of the military importance of that island in all
attacks on Canada.

learn their names. The lake, on an average, may be six miles broad; in some places it is above fifteen miles wide, particularly about Cumberland bay and Schuyler's island; but in others it is not three miles, and in the narrows not above a mile and a half, to judge by the eye. As you go down the lake, the mountains which hem it in on the east and west extend themselves wider, and leave a greater extent of fine level land between them and the lake on each shore. Some of these mountains are remarkably high. In many places, on or near their tops, the snow still remains. They form several picturesque views, and contribute much, in my opinion, to the beauty of the lake. The snow not dissolving, in their latitude, at the end of April, is a proof of their height:—the distance at which some of these mountains are visible is a still stronger proof. Several of them may be distinctly seen from Montreal, which can not be at a less distance from the most remote than seventy or eighty miles, and, I am inclined to think, considerably further. If America should succeed, and establish liberty throughout this part of the continent, I have not the least doubt that the lands bordering on Lake Champlain will be very valuable in a short time, and that great trade will be carried on over Lake Champlain, between Canada and New York. An easy

water communication may be opened, at no great
expense, (if General Schuyler be not mistaken,)
between the cities of New York, Montreal, and
Quebec, and several other places in Canada.
Richelieu, or *Sorel river*, from *Isle aux Têtes* to
St. John's, would be esteemed a large river even
in Maryland. The navigation of it between those
places is good, for the current is not so strong
as not to be stemmed with oars, or a wind. At
St. John's the current is very rapid, and continues so, sometimes more, sometimes less, to
Chamblay,—distant twelve miles from St. John's.
Opposite St. John's, I think the river is half a
mile wide.

The fortifications of St. John's were not injured
by the siege;—they consist of earth ramparts,
enclosed by a ditch filled with water; palisadoes,
closely joined together, are fastened at the base
of the ramparts, and confined by the weight of
them projecting half way over the ditch, to prevent an escalade. There are, properly speaking,
two forts, built around some houses, which were
converted into magazines and barracks;—the
communication between the two is secured by a
strong enclosure of large stakes driven deep into
the ground, and as close as they can stand
together. A ditch runs along this fence. The
houses within the forts suffered much from our
batteries which surrounded the forts, but the

12

cannon was not heavy enough to make any
impression on the works. Want of ammunition
and provisions, and the inclemency of the season,
obliged the garrison to surrender; for the soldiers were constrained to hide themselves in the
cellars, which are bomb-proof, or lie behind the
mounds of earth thrown up within the forts,
exposed to the severity of the cold and rains, or
run the risk of having their brains beaten out in
the houses by our shot, or by a fragment of the
walls and timbers, and bursting of the bombs.
As you go down the river from *Point au Fer* to
St. John's, you have a distant and beautiful prospect of the mountains on either side of the lake.
After passing *Isle aux Noix*, you have a fine
view of the mountain of Chamblay, on the top
of which is a lake stored with excellent trout
and perch. Having despatched a messenger to
Montreal for carriages for ourselves and baggage,
we crossed the river to go to a tavern on the
east side of the river, about a mile from the
fort. The house belongs to Colonel Hazen, and
has greatly suffered by the neighborhood of the
troops. There is scarcely a whole pane of glass
in the house, the window-shutters and doors are
destroyed, and the hinges stolen; in short, it
appears a perfect wreck. This tavern is kept by
a French woman, married to one Donaho, now a
prisoner in Pennsylvania.

28th. We remained at Colonel Hazen's house. Several batteaux with troops arrived this day and yesterday evening from Ticonderoga, and most of them fell down the river this day to Chamblay. The land appears to be very fertile, and well adapted to pasture; the grass began to grow fast, although the frost was not then out of the ground, the surface only being thawed.[1]

29th. Left Colonel Hazen's house; crossed over to St. John's, where we found our *calèches* ready to receive us. After an hour's stay spent in getting our baggage into the carts, and securing the remainder,—which, for want of carts, we were obliged to leave behind us,—we set off from St. John's for *La Prairie*, distant eighteen miles. I never travelled through worse roads, or in worse carriages. The country is one continued plain from St. John's to *La Prairie*, and two-thirds of the way uncultivated, though deserving the highest cultivation. About five or six miles from *La Prairie* you meet with houses and ploughed lands, interspersed with meadows, which extend as far as you can see;—all this tract of land is capable of being turned into fine meadow, and when the country becomes more populous, and enjoys a good government, I doubt not it will be all

1 Immediately on the arrival of the commissioners at Montreal, Mr. John Carroll addressed a letter to his mother, dated 1st May, giving an interesting account of their journey to Canada. The reader will find it in the American Archives, vol. v, p. 1158.

drained and made into excellent meadow or pasturage. Without draining, it will be impossible to cultivate it in any way. You have no view of the St. Lawrence, or of Montreal, until you come within three or four miles of *La Prairie*. At *La Prairie* the view of the town and the river, and the island of Montreal, together with the houses on the eastern side of the St. Lawrence, form a beautiful prospect. As far as the view extends down the river, you discern houses on either side of it, which are not divided from each other by more than four acres, and commonly by not more than two. From *La Prairie* you go slanting down the river to Montreal; this passage is computed six miles, though the river, in a direct line across from the eastern shore to the town, is not more than three miles. Ships of three hundred tons can come up to Montreal; but they can not get up above the town, or even abreast of it. The river where we crossed is filled with rocks and shoals, which occasion a very rapid current in several places. We were received by GENERAL ARNOLD, on our landing, in the most polite and friendly manner; conducted to headquarters, where a genteel company of ladies and gentlemen had assembled to welcome our arrival. As we went from the landing place to the general's house, the cannon of the citadel fired in compliment to us as the commissioners

of congress. We supped at that general's, and
after supper were conducted, by the general and
other gentlemen, to our lodgings,—the house of
Mr. Thomas Walker,—the best built, and perhaps the best furnished in this town.[1]

May 11th. Dr. Franklin left Montreal to-day
to go to St. John's, and from thence to congress.
The doctor's declining state of health, and the
bad prospect of our affairs in Canada, made him
take this resolution.[2]

[1] See Arnold's letter to Schuyler, Montreal, April 30, 1776.—*Archives,*
vol. v, p. 1155. And see also, Commissioners' letter to Congress, dated
Montreal, 1 May, 1776, with the memorandum of the council of war as
to fortifying Jaques Cartier and the falls of Richelieu, and the building
of six gondolas.—*American Archives,* vol. v, p. 1166.

[2] Dr. Franklin's health (as he had predicted at the outset) was im-
paired by the hardships of this journey. After being a fortnight at
Montreal, he set out homewards with Mr. John Carroll, who afterwards became the first Roman Catholic Archbishop of the United
States. With some difficulty they reached Albany, whence they came
to New York in a private carriage furnished by General Schuyler.
In a letter, dated at New York on the 27th of May, he thanks General Schuyler and his wife for their attention to his comforts; and is
glad that he did not pursue his original intention of taking the general's
sulky and driving over the stones and gullies, in which he should probably have overset and broken his bones.
In a letter of the same date, "to the Commissioners in Canada," he
informs his friends of his arrival, and rather petulantly says that they
"left Mrs. Walker with her husband at Albany, from whence we came
down by land. We passed him on Lake Champlain ; but he, returning,
overtook us at Saratoga, *when they both took such liberties in taunting at
our conduct in Canada, that it came almost to a quarrel.* We continued
our care of her, however, and landed her safe in Albany, with her three
wagon loads of baggage, *brought thither without putting her to any expense,* and parted civilly though coldly. *I think they both have an excellent talent at making themselves enemies, and I believe, live where they
will, they will never be long without them.*" The Walkers are probably
the family alluded to in the journal on the 29th of May.—*Works of
Franklin,* vol. i, p. 404, and vol. viii, pp. 182, 183, Sparks's edition.

12th. We set off from Montreal to go to *La Prairie.* Mr. John Carroll went to join Dr. Franklin at St. John's, from whence they sailed the 13th.[1]

13th. I went to St. John's to examine into the state of that garrison, and of the batteaux. There I met with General Thompson and Colonel Sinclair, with part of Thompson's brigade. That evening I went with them down the Sorel to Chamblay. Major Wood and myself remained in the boat when we got to St. Thérèse, where the rapids begin and continue, with some interruptions, to Chamblay. Flat bottomed boats may go down these rapids in the spring of the year, when the water is high;— even a large *gondola* passed down them this spring; but it would be very difficult, if not impossible, to bring a *gondola* up against the stream. I much question whether the batteaux could be brought up; certain it is that the labor of towing them up, or setting them up the current with setting poles,

---

[1] Franklin did not forget the kind attentions of the Rev. John Carroll during this journey; nor did he fail to appreciate the virtues and intellectual cultivation of that excellent clergyman. The following extract from the doctor's private journal at Passy in 1784, shows that he thought of him constantly, and pressed his claims for the highest dignity of the church in our confederacy.

"*July 1st*, (*1784*.)—The pope's nuncio called, and acquainted me that the pope had, on my recommendation, appointed Mr. John Carroll superior of the Catholic clergy in America, with many powers of bishop; and that, probably, he would be made a bishop, *in partibus*, before the end of the year."—See *Works of Franklin*, vol. i, p. 581, Sparks's edition.

Painted by J. Paul.　　　　　　Eng.ᵈ by H.B.Hall.

JOHN CARROLL, D.D.

would be greater, and take much more time, than carting them over the carrying place from Chamblay to within three miles of St. Thérèse. All our batteaux which shoot the rapids and go down the Sorel to Chamblay and that are brought up again to St. John's, are carted over the carrying place on frames constructed for the purpose. It was proposed by some to bring a *gondola*, built at Chamblay, over land three miles into the Sorel, three miles below St. Thérèse; others were of opinion it could be more easily towed up over the rapids. *Chamblay fort* is a large square stone building, with square towers at each angle, a place intended only as a protection against the savages. I saw the holes made by a six pounder, when it was taken by Major Brown. Major Stafford might have held out against the force which besieged him at least for some days, in which time he would probably have been relieved by Carleton. But, by Carleton's subsequent behaviour, when he made an attempt to go to the relief of St. John's, I much question whether he would have taken more effectual measures to rescue Stafford. The taking of Chamblay occasioned the taking of St. John's; against the latter we should not have succeeded without the six tons of gunpowder taken in the former.

14th. I returned to Montreal by *La Prairie;* the country between Chamblay and *La Prairie* is extremely fine and level, abounding with most excellent meadow-ground as you approach the St. Lawrence, with rich arable land round about Chamblay. The country lying between the St. Lawrence and the Sorel is the best part of Canada, and produces the most and best wheat. In the year 1771 four hundred and seventy-one thousand bushels of wheat were exported out of Canada, of which two-thirds, it is computed, were made in the Sorel district.[1]

21st. This day Mr. Chase set off with me for the mouth of the Sorel; we embarked from Montreal in one of our batteaux, and went in it as far as the point of land on the north shore of the St. Lawrence, opposite to the northern extremity of the Island of Montreal; here, the wind being against us, we took post and travelled on the north side of the St. Lawrence as low down as *La Nore,* where we got into a canoe, and were paddled down and across the St. Lawrence to our camp at the mouth of the Sorel;— it was a perfect calm, the distance is computed at nine miles. The country on each side the St.

---

[1] The commissioners wrote to congress from Montreal on the 8th of May.—See *American Archives,* vol. v, p. 1237. On May 10th from same place.—See *American Archives,* vol. vi, p. 450. And again on the 16th May.—*Id.* p. 482.

Lawrence is level, rich, and thickly seated; indeed, so thickly seated, that the houses form almost one continued row. In going from *La Nore* to the mouth of the Sorel, we passed by Brown's battery (as it is called), although it never had a cannon mounted on it. To this battery without cannon, and to a single gondola, ten or twelve vessels, under the command of Colonel Prescott, surrendered. Major Brown, when the vessels came near to his battery, sent an officer on board requesting Prescott to send another on shore to view his works. It is difficult to determine which was greatest, the impudence of Brown in demanding a surrender, or the cowardice of the officer who, going back to Prescott, represented the difficulty of passing the battery so great and hazardous, that Prescott and all his officers chose to capitulate. Brown requested the officer who went on shore to wait a little until he saw the two thirty-two pounders, which were within a half a mile, coming from Chamblay;—says he, "If you should chance to escape this battery, which is my small battery, I have a grand battery at the mouth of the Sorel, which will infallibly sink all your vessels." His grand battery was as badly provided with cannon as his little battery, for not a single gun was mounted on either. This Prescott treated our prisoners with great insolence and brutality. His

13

behaviour justifies the old observation, that cowards are generally cruel. We found the discipline of our camp very remiss, and every thing in confusion;—General Thomas had but lately resigned the command to Thompson, by whose activity things were soon put on a better footing.

22d. We left our camp and travelled by land along the eastern bank of the Sorel. At five or six miles from the mouth of the Sorel the country grows rich, and continues so all the way to Chamblay. Near the mouth of the river it is very sandy. This part of the country is very populous, the villages are large and neat, and joined together by a continued range of single houses, chiefly farmers' houses. These are the rich men in Canada: the *seignieurs* are in general poor. They were constrained by the ordinances of the king of France to lease their lands for ever, reserving two dollars for every ninety acres, and some other trifling perquisites, as tolls for grinding wheat; the tenants being obliged to have their wheat ground at their *seignieurs'* mills. It is conjectured that the farmers in Canada can not be possessed of less than a million sterling, in specie;—they hoard up their money to portion their children;—they neither let it out at interest, nor expend it in the purchase of lands. Before we left the camp we ordered a detachment up to Montreal, under the command of Colonel De

Haas, consisting of near four hundred men, to reinforce General Arnold, and, in conjunction, to drive off a party of the eighth regiment, who, with three hundred and fifty savages, and some Canadians, had taken our post at the Cedars, through the cowardice of Major Butterfield,[1] and had advanced, on the 25th instant, within fifteen miles of Montreal.

23d. We got early this morning to Chamblay, where we found all things in much confusion, extreme disorder, and negligence, our credit sunk, and no money to retrieve it with. We were obliged to pay three silver dollars for the carriage of three barrels of gunpowder from Little Chamblay river to Longueil, the officer who commanded the guard not having a single shilling.

24th. Colonel De Haas's detachment got into Montreal this evening; the day before, we also arrived there, having crossed the St. Lawrence in a canoe from Longueil.

25th. In the evening of this day Colonel De Haas's detachment marched out of Montreal to join General Arnold at La Chine; they were

---

[1] Arnold had left Quebec on account of his suffering from a severe wound, but more probably in consequence of his jealousy and discontent with General Wooster. At Montreal he was again in command, and, for the results of his course after the disaster at the Cedars, the reader is referred to his life, in Sparks's American Biography, vol. iii, p. 56, et seq.

At the Cedars, nearly four hundred men surrendered, by a disgraceful capitulation, and a hundred more were barbarously murdered by savages.

detained from want of many necessaries, which we were obliged to procure for them, General Wooster being without money, or pretending to be so.[1] The enemy, hearing from our enemies in Montreal, of this reinforcement, had retreated precipitately to Fort St. Anne's, at the southern extremity of the Island of Montreal, and from thence had crossed over to *Quinze Chiens*, on the north side of the St. Lawrence.

29th. We left Montreal this day at three o'clock,[2] to go to Chamblay, to be present at a

[1] In a letter from the Commissioners to Congress, dated at Montreal on the 27th May, '76, they deal with General Wooster in unmeasured terms. "General Thomas," they say, "is now at Chamblay under the small-pox. Being taken with that disorder, he left the camp at Sorel, and wrote to General Wooster to come and take command. When the interest of our country and the safety of your army are at stake, we think it very improper to conceal our sentiments, either with regard to persons or things. General Wooster is, in our opinion, unfit—totally unfit—to command your army and conduct the war. We have, hitherto, prevailed on him to remain in Montreal. His stay in this colony is unnecessary, and even prejudicial to our affairs. We would therefore humbly advise his recall."—*MS. letter in the State department at Washington.* It is published by Mr. Force in the sixth volume of the American Archives, at p. 589.

Wooster requested an inquiry into his conduct as commander of the forces in Canada. The matter was referred by congress to a committee, which, upon full investigation, declared that nothing censurable appeared against him.—See *Journals of Congress, August 17th, 1776.* He resigned his commission in the continental army, and was appointed first major-general of the Connecticut militia.—See *Sparks's Life and Writings of Washington,* vol. iii, p. 412, *in note.*

Wooster was killed in 1777, in a spirited action between the Connecticut troops and the English force under Governor Tryon, near Danbury.

[2] See letter from the Commissioners to Congress, dated 27 May, 1776, in the sixth volume of American Archives, p. 590. This is their last letter from Canada, and is very valuable, as containing a very full report of the state of affairs in that province, and the condition of the army. It has been freely extracted from in the introductory memoir.

council of war of the generals and field-officers, for concerting the operations of the campaign.

30th. The council of war was held this day, and determined to maintain possession of the country between the St. Lawrence and Sorel, if possible;—in the meantime to dispose matters so as to make an orderly retreat out of Canada.

31st. Set off from Chamblay for St. John's;— all things there in confusion:— slept at Mrs. Donaho's.

June 1st. Crossed over this morning to St. John's, where General Sullivan, with fourteen hundred men, had arrived in the night of the 31st past; saw them all under arms. It began to rain at nine o'clock, and continued raining very hard until late in the evening;— slept at Donaho's.

2d. Crossed over again to the camp; took leave of General Sullivan, and sailed from St. John's at six this morning, with a fair wind;—got to *Point au Fer* at one o'clock;—got to Cumberland head about seven o'clock, P. M.; set off from thence about nine, and rowed all night. We divided our boat's crew into two watches.

3d. Breakfasted at Willsborough; rowed on and received despatches by Major Hickes; got to Crown Point half-past six o'clock, P. M. Set off at eight, rowed all night, and arrived at one o'clock in the night at Ticonderoga, where we found General Schuyler.

4th. Set off this morning at five with General Schuyler, for Skeenesborough, and got there by two o'clock. The lake, as you approach Skeenesborough, grows narrower and shallower; indeed, within five or six miles of Skeenesborough, it has all the appearance of a river. We hauled our batteau over the carrying place at Skeenesborough into Wood creek. This carrying place is not above three hundred feet across; a lock may be made for two hundred pounds at Skeenesborough, by which means a continued navigation would be effected for batteaux from one Chesshire's into Lake Champlain. Major Skene has built a saw-mill, grist mill, and a forge at the entrance of Wood creek into Lake Champlain. Set off from Skeenesborough at four o'clock, rowed up Wood creek ten miles, to one Boyle's, here we lay all night on board our boat.

5th. Set off at three in the morning, and continued rowing up the creek to one Chesshire's. This man lives near Fort Ann, built by Governor Nicholson in 1709. The distance from Skeenesborough to Chesshire's, is twenty-two miles,—by land, fourteen only; from this it appears that Wood creek has many windings, in fact, I never saw a more serpentine river. The navigation is somewhat obstructed by trees drifted and piled across the creek; however, we met with little difficulty but in one place, where we were obliged to quit our boat, and carry it through a narrow gut, which was soon performed by our crew. Two hundred men would clear this creek and remove every obstruction in six days' time. This measure has been recommended by the commissioners to congress, and congress has complied with the recommendation, and orders will soon be given to General Schuyler to clear it, and render the navigation easy.

I set off with General Schuyler, on foot, from Chesshire's, at one o'clock; walked seven miles, and then met horses coming from Jones's to us. Jones's house is distant nine miles from Chesshire's. We dined at Jones's, and rode, after dinner, to Fort Edward;—the distance is computed four miles;—Mr. Chase joined us this evening. He took the lower road and was obliged to walk part of the way.

6th. Parted with General Schuyler this morning; he returned to Fort George on Lake George. We rode to Saratoga, where we got by seven o'clock, but did not find the amiable family at home. We were constrained to remain here all this day, waiting the arrival of our servants and baggage.

7th. Our servants and baggage being come up, we left Saratoga this morning at nine; took boat and went down Hudson's river, through all the rapids, to Albany. The distance is computed thirty-six miles. We arrived at Albany half an hour past five. At six o'clock we set off for New York in a sloop: which we luckily found ready to sail; got that evening and night twenty-four miles from Albany.

8th. Found ourselves, this morning, twenty-four miles from Albany;—at seven in the morning wind breezed up, had a fine gale, and got below the highlands;—a very great run.

9th. Arrived at New York at one o'clock, P. M.; Waited on General Washington at Motier's;—saw Generals Gates and Putnam, and my old acquaintance and friend, Mr. Moylan. About six o'clock in the evening got into General Washington's barge, in company with Lord Stirling,[1] and was rowed round by Staten Island and the Kilns, within two miles of Elizabeth-town, where we got by ten at night.

10th. Set off from Elizabeth-town half-past five. Got to Bristol at eight o'clock, P. M.:—at nine, embarked in our boats, and were rowed down the Delaware to Philadelphia, where we arrived at two o'clock in the night.

---

[1] Lord Stirling was a brigadier-general in the American army, and stationed at New York, where he had command for a short time, after the departure of General Lee.—See *Washington's Writings,* vol. iii, p. 318; and *Franklin's Writings,* vol. viii, p. 180, *note,* (*Sparks's Edition.*) On the 27th of March, 1776, Franklin had apprised him by letter of the proposed journey to Canada, and desired him to procure lodgings for the party in New York, as well as to engage a sloop to take them up the river to Albany.

AUTOBIOGRAPHIC SKETCH

OF

CHARLES CARROLL OF CARROLLTON.

On the 28th of July, 1816, Mr. Joseph Delaplaine, editor and publisher at that time of "The Repository," wrote to Mr. Carroll thanking him for his consent to sit to Mr. King, the artist, for a portrait which Mr. Delaplaine desired to have. At the conclusion of his letter, which fills the first side of a quarto sheet, the writer adds: "I beg you, Sir, to furnish me with a few facts of your Life—Birth—Parentage—Education—Offices—Profession—Correspondence with General Washington, and any facts you may be pleased to furnish."

On the receipt of this, Mr. Carroll, then near entering on his eightieth year,—turned over the first page of this letter, and on the two inner pages, set down, in a clear but slightly trembling hand, the following draft, which is preserved in my collection of Letters of the Signers of the Declaration of Independence.

"Doughoragan, 21 Aug., 1816.

"Sir:

"I received this day your letter of the 28th past, and the first half volume of your Repository, for which I hope my agent Mr. James Neilson, in Baltimore, has accounted with your agent Mr. Philson. My letter of 6th instant in answer to Mr. King's of the 29th July, informed him I should be in Baltimore about the 20th December and remain there during the winter, when I will sit to him for my portrait at any place in that city he may appoint.

"I was born at Annapolis in September, 1737; on the 19th of next month I shall enter into my 80th year. I was sent by my father when about 11 years of age to St. Omer's for my education, where I remained about 6 years; from thence I went, by his direction, to a College at Rheims, and after remaining at that College a year, I went to the College of Louis le Grand at Paris; in all of these Colleges the students were taught by the Jesuites.

"In 1758 or 1759, I went to England and studied law in the Inner Temple 3 or 4 years, not with a professional view; and returned to my native country in 1765, after an absence of about 18 years.

"On the breaking out of our revolution I took a decided part in support of the rights of this country; was elected a member of the Committee of Safety established by the legislature; was a member of the Convention which formed the constitution of this State. The journals of Congress will show how long I was a member of that body during the revolution.

"With Dr. Franklin and Mr. Samuel Chase, I was appointed a Commissioner to Canada. I was elected a member of the Senate at the first session of Congress under the present Con-

federation:—though well acquainted with General Washington,
— and I flatter myself in his confidence,—few letters passed
between us; one, having reference to the opposition made to the
Treaty concluded by Mr. Jay, has been repeatedly published in
the newspapers, and perhaps you may have seen it; that letter
is no longer in my possession.

"My Grandfather came to Maryland in the year preceding the
revolution in England, terminated by the dethronement of James
the Second. My mother was daughter of Mr. Clement Brooke,
a gentleman of respectable family in Prince George's County.—
I have given you, Sir, in compliance with your request, all the
incidents of my public life and of my education, and remain, with
respect,

"Y^r most hum: Servt

"CHARLES CARROLL OF CARROLLTON."

The letter from Mr. Delaplaine before referred to, on the inner
pages of which the above was written, is endorsed in Mr. Carroll's handwriting:

"1816: August 28

"Joseph Delaplaine's Letter:

"received the 21 August and answered same day:

"see my answer within."

This particularity is interesting as showing the promptness
with which Mr. Carroll always attended to business, and especially to his correspondence, many specimens of which are in my
possession. Another interesting biographical scrap in my collection, is contained in an envelope endorsed by Mr. Carroll's

father: "A Character of my Son: By Mr. Jenison his Master;" beneath which the modest son has written:

"I fear this letter was dictated by Mr. Jenison's partiality to me. I never found till this day (27th July, 1782) that he ever wrote to my Father about me."

The character is as follows:

"Tho' I am not in a disposition of Writing Letters, having lost this morning the finest young man, in every respect, that ever enter'd the House, you will, perhaps, afterwards, have the pleasure of assuring yourself by experience that I've not exaggerated Charles Carroll's character in the foregoing lines. The Captain will be able to give you, I hope, a satisfactory account of him. 'Tis very natural I should regret the loss of one who during the whole time he was under my care, never deserv'd, on any account, a single harsh word, and whose sweet temper rendered him equally agreeable both to equals and superiors, without ever making him degenerate into the mean character of a favorite which he always justly despis'd. His application to his Book and Devotions was constant and unchangeable, nor could we perceive the least difference in his conduct even after having read the news of his destination, which, you know, is very usual with young people here. This short character I owe to his deserts;—prejudice, I am convinc'd, has no share in it, as I find the public voice confirms my private sentiments. Both inclination and justice prompt me to say more, yet I rather chuse to leave the rest to Captain Carroll to inform you of by word of mouth."

BRANTZ MAYER,

EDITOR.

LETTER FROM REV'D JOHN CARROLL

(Afterwards Archbishop of Baltimore)

TO CHARLES CARROLL, Esq.,

Father of Charles Carroll of Carrollton.

————————

"Philadelphia, *June 2d, 1776.*

"Hon⁴ Dʳ Sʳ

"I arrived at this place the day before yesterday in company with Dr. Franklin. Cousin Charles and Mr. Chace left Montreal with me on the 12th of May, that they might not be in any danger from a frigate running up the River and getting between them and the Eastern shore of S. Lawrence. As Dr. Franklin determined to return to Philadelphia, on account of his health, I resolved to accompany him, seeing it was out of my power to be of any service after the Commissioners had thought it advisable for them to leave Montreal. Your Son and Mr. Chace proposed staying at S. John's or in that neighbourhood, till they should know whether our army would keep post at De Chambeau; and the former desired me to give you notice of his being safe and well. Since I left him it has not been in my power to do it before this day, as we unfortunately chanced to come to every post town on our road sometimes a day, sometimes a few hours too late for the mail. When I left him he expected to

109

follow us in a few days: but Mr. Hancock tells me that if an express sent some days since from Congress, reaches them before they have left Canada, he is of opinion they will continue there for some time.   I shall set out from hence, next week and propose doing myself the pleasure of calling at Elk-ridge.   My aff^te and respectful compl^ts to Mrs. Darnall and Carroll with love to Polley.   Nothing new from Canada, nor indeed any advices at all since we left it.   Great divisions here between the contending parties.   I have presumed to trouble you to forward the inclosed and remain

"Hon^d D^r S^r

"Y^r aff^te kinsman and hum Sev^t

"J. CARROLL."

"Ten tons of powder,
"500 small arms came in *yesterday.*

"Cos^n Charles rece^d large packets of letters from you a few days before we left Montreal."

" To Charles Carroll Senr Esqre
"to the care of Mr Wm Lux
" Baltimore
"free J. Carroll." [1]

1 Original MS. in the Archives of the Maryland Historical Society.